21世纪旅游英语系列教材

酒店英语(视听版)

(第二版)

Hotel English
An Audio-visual Version
(Second Edition)

朱 华 主编

图书在版编目(CIP)数据

酒店英语:视听版 / 朱华主编. —2版. —北京:北京大学出版社,2021.9
21世纪旅游英语系列教材
ISBN 978-7-301-32428-8

Ⅰ.①酒⋯ Ⅱ.①朱⋯ Ⅲ.①饭店–英语–高等学校–教材 Ⅳ.①F719.2

中国版本图书馆CIP数据核字(2021)第171878号

书　　　名	酒店英语(视听版)(第二版) JIUDIAN YINGYU (SHITING BAN) (DI-ER BAN)
著作责任者	朱　华　主编
责 任 编 辑	李　颖
标 准 书 号	ISBN 978-7-301-32428-8
出 版 发 行	北京大学出版社
地　　　址	北京市海淀区成府路205号　100871
网　　　址	http://www.pup.cn　新浪微博:@北京大学出版社
电 子 邮 箱	编辑部 pupwaiwen@pup.cn　总编室 zpup@pup.cn
电　　　话	邮购部 010-62752015　发行部 010-62750672　编辑部 010-62759634
印 刷 者	三河市博文印刷有限公司
经 销 者	新华书店
	787毫米×1092毫米　16开本　12.75印张　413千字 2014年8月第1版 2021年9月第2版　2024年5月第4次印刷
定　　　价	52.00元

未经许可,不得以任何方式复制或抄袭本书之部分或全部内容。
版权所有,侵权必究
举报电话: 010-62752024　电子邮箱: fd@pup.cn
图书如有印装质量问题,请与出版部联系,电话: 010-62756370

本教材音视频免费下载地址:www.pup.cn/下载中心

《酒店英语(视听版)》(第二版)

尊敬的老师：

您好！

为了方便您更好地使用本教材，获得最佳教学效果，我们特向使用该书作为教材的教师赠送本教材配套课件资料。如有需要，请完整填写"教师联系表"并加盖所在单位系(院)公章，免费向出版社索取。

北京大学出版社

教 师 联 系 表

教材名称	《酒店英语(视听版)》(第二版)					
姓名：		性别：		职务：		职称：
E-mail：		联系电话：			邮政编码：	
供职学校：			所在院系：			
						（章）
学校地址：						
教学科目与年级：			班级人数：			
通信地址：						

填写完毕后，请将此表邮寄给我们，我们将为您免费寄送本教材配套资料，谢谢！

北京市海淀区成府路205号
北京大学出版社外语编辑部　李　颖
邮政编码：100871
电子邮箱：evalee1770@sina.com

邮 购 部 电 话：010-62534449
市场营销部电话：010-62750672
外语编辑部电话：010-62754382

前　言

　　《酒店英语(视听版)》(第二版)听、说、练紧密结合,通过不同的酒店工作场景学习酒店专业知识,培养学生运用酒店英语进行工作交流的能力。本教材将酒店专业知识和专门用途英语相结合,减少了企业二次培训成本。第二版为酒店英语视、听、说立体化培训教材,集文字、图形、图像、音频、视频为一体,视听说结合,还原酒店工作场景,让学生在真实的环境中学习酒店英语和相关专业知识。第二版有以下特点:

　　1. 教材将酒店主要业务与英语技能同步讲授,学生学完一章后即可掌握本章节酒店相关技能和工作程序。
　　2. 融入酒店实训内容和职业资格认证培训内容,将学历教育和职业教育结合起来,将职业培训纳入学历教育中。
　　3. 视、听、说、练有机结合,通过酒店视频、音频再现,让学生身临其境,模拟学习不同酒店场景中的语言和技能。
　　4. 教材配有酒店实训视频,并配文字资料,教师可根据不同学习对象和内容难易情况,选择视频教学或文字教学,也可合二为一。

　　《酒店英语(视听版)》(第二版)采用 MES(Modules of Employable Skill)模块式教学设计。任课教师可以根据授课对象和课时数对教学内容进行分拆和整合。需要课件的老师可填写教师联系表从北京大学出版社领取,或致函 ernestzhu@126 索取。

朱　华

Contents 目 录

Chapter 1 Reservation 预订 1

Chapter 2 Registration 入住登记 13

Chapter 3 Concierge 礼宾服务 24

Chapter 4 Private Branch Exchange 总机 35

Chapter 5 Check-out 退房 45

Chapter 6 Housekeeping 客房部 56

Chapter 7 Food and Beverage 餐饮服务 70

Chapter 8 Western Food 西式餐点 81

Chapter 9 Western Beverage 西餐酒水 91

Chapter 10 Chinese Food 中式餐点 101

Chapter 11 Chinese Tea and Alcohol 中国茶和酒 114

Chapter 12 Room Service 送餐服务 125

Chapter 13 Banquet Service 宴会服务 134

Chapter 14 Recreational Activities 娱乐活动 146

Chapter 15 Shopping Arcade 购物中心 157

Chapter 16 Complaints Settlement 处理投诉 169

Appendices 附录 ... 180

- Appendix 1　客房设施和日用品 ... 180
- Appendix 2　中餐英文菜名 ... 181
- Appendix 3　西餐英文菜名 ... 184
- Appendix 4　外国酒名 ... 187
- Appendix 5　中国酒名 ... 188
- Appendix 6　中国茶和茶具 ... 191
- Appendix 7　中餐餐具 ... 193
- Appendix 8　西餐餐具 ... 194

Bibliography 参考文献 ... 195

Chapter 1
Reservation
预 订

Major Topics 一、酒店知识：Reservation with Computer Software 用电脑软件预订房间
二、酒店员工：Reservation Manager 预订经理
　　　　　　　Reservationist 预订员
　　　　　　　Revenue Manager 收益经理
三、酒店视频：Hidden Fees of a Hotel 酒店的隐蔽费用
四、酒店对话：Scenario 1: Take Down Reservations 记录预订
　　　　　　　Scenario 2: Keep Updates 保持更新
　　　　　　　Scenario 3: Ask for a Discount 要求折扣
　　　　　　　Scenario 4: Make a Business Reservation 商务预订
五、巩固练习

This chapter concentrates on the reservation department. In *Part One*, you'll read ABC about reservation with computer software as a warming-up exercise. In *Part Two*, job description of working staff is provided for you to have some basics about the responsibility of each job at Reception. In *Part Three*, you'll watch a short video about the hidden fees of a hotel you may have neglected when you make a reservation. In the next section, *Part Four* will provide some situational dialogues for you to practice the reservation skills based on different scenarios in the hotel. *Part Five* includes additional exercises to enhance your knowledge and skills of the reservation task.

Part One ABC for Hotel
一、酒店知识

Reservation with Computer Software 用电脑软件预订房间

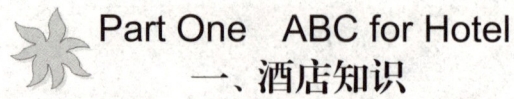

hospitality /ˌhɒspɪˈtæləti/ *n.* 招待业(如旅馆、饭店等)
automate /ˈɔːtəmeɪt/ *v.* 自动化
manipulate /məˈnɪpjʊleɪt/ *v.* 操作
availability /əˌveɪləˈbɪləti/ *n.* 可用率
facilitate /fəˈsɪlɪteɪt/ *v.* 促进
interface /ˈɪntəfeɪs/ *n.* 界面
folio /ˈfəʊlɪəʊ/ *n.* 页码;档案
track /træk/ *n.* 轨迹
integrate /ˈɪntɪgreɪt/ *v.* 整合
beforehand /bɪˈfɔːhænd/ *adv.* 事先
intuitive /ɪnˈtjuːɪtɪv/ *adj.* 直觉的
multiple /ˈmʌltɪpl/ *adj.* 多样的

With the growing competition in the hospitality industry, the need for effective and efficient management of the hotels, motels, and lodges is being felt by their owners. Hotel reservation software is truly a boon for the hoteliers looking to provide 100% customer satisfaction without having to work really hard for the same. The software not only helps to automate the process of reservation in the hotel, but also helps the efficient management of the same.

Whether it is making reservations, billing or keeping track of the customers, the hotel software provides everything at just a few mouse clicks. This software is principally created to suit the requirement of the hotel management and can be easily installed and manipulated according to the specific need of the hotel. Software for hotels primarily runs on Windows, but can be developed to suit user requirements. The functions performed by such software include room reservations, customer check-in and check-out, the integrated statement for all customers and hotel billing. Benefits that can be derived from such an application include:

- save the processing time;
- easy and quick reservation;
- keeping track of customers' information.

The most prominent software is the hotel reservation software, which features dedicated room booking and reservation utilities. It helps to store the information regarding room availability and expected duration of stay of the occupier. This will help the customer to have a beforehand report on the availability of rooms and booking status. Nowadays, hotel reservation system is integrated with online access provisions, facilitates users with online booking and reservations, and provides a unique and intuitive interface improving the way that the web is used. Other additional functions include:

- ♨ guest room reservation;
- ♨ group operations and management;
- ♨ authorization of credit card;
- ♨ seasonal rates setups;
- ♨ multiple currency payments;
- ♨ daily room and revenue report generation;
- ♨ guest arrival list and guest folio;
- ♨ receipt generation.

The hotel software can be employed in front desk department, housekeeping department, reservation department and accounts department of a hotel in order to organize proper hotel activities and day-to-day operations. This capability offers a wide range of adaptability that satisfies both the customers and hotel personnel.

Based on the above passage, decide whether the following statements are true or false. Write T for true and F for false.

1. _____ The hotel reservation software can be used in many departments, including front desk, F&B and conference.
2. _____ The hotel reservation software can not only suit Windows system, but also be tailored to other requirements.
3. _____ The hotel reservation software is designed to help both reservationists and hotel customers.
4. _____ Reservationists are able to access internet booking through the hotel reservation software.

Part Two Working Staff
二、酒店员工

1 Listen to the job description of each one in the department, correct the mistakes and put the right ones in the blanks.

(1) **Reservation Manager** works closely with the hotel sales team to change room rates depending on seasonal demands and revenue requirements.

To liaise with central reservations to regulate new rate plans and promotion.
To liaise with travel agents, the Revenue Manager and the Room Division Manager.
To assist the sales team in fixing their rates.
To maintain the in-house reservation systems.
To forecast guest cycle.
In smaller hotels they may be directly involved with room sales.

a. _____
b. _____

中文提示:

  预订经理：与酒店销售部紧密合作，根据季节需要和销售额要求而改变房价。预订经理与中央预订联络沟通，制定新的价格和促销计划；与旅游中介、收益经理和房务经理联络；协助销售部制定价格；维护酒店内预订系统；预测营业额；在一些较小的酒店还需要直接参与客房销售。

(2) **Reservationist** makes and confirms customer reservations, reports to Reservation Manager.
  To deal with guests over the telephone.
  To take and output data.
  To negotiate rates in hotels.
  To up-sell, or offer a less expensive house to the customer.
   a. _____
   b. _____
  中文提示:

  预订员：制定和确认顾客的预定，向预订经理负责。主要职责有：处理顾客电话预订；制定和输入预订信息；与顾客协商房价；推销或为顾客提供价格更贵的房间。

(3) **Revenue Manager** tracks the space rates of bedrooms and conferences offered by competitors, and makes sure rooms are sold at the right price and at the right time to the right people.
  To analyze booking patterns and market trends.
  To monitor competitor's performance.
  To carry out effective loyalty management.
  To initiate promotions to generate business at critical moments.
  To forecast cash flow.
  To liaise with the sales teams, reception and the General Manager.
   a. _____
   b. _____
  中文提示:

  收益经理：追踪竞争对手的房价和会议场所的价格，确保本酒店的房间以恰当的价格，在恰当的时间卖给恰当的顾客。主要职责有：分析预订情况和市场趋势；监视竞争者销售状况；有效地进行收益管理；在关键时刻促销；预测收益；并与销售部、接待处和总经理保持联络。

② Listen again and discuss the job description of the position you wish to hold in your career.

Part Three Video for the Hotel
三、酒店视频

Hidden Fees of a Hotel 酒店的隐蔽费用

Word Tips

occupancy /ˈɒkjʊpənsɪ/ n. 占用
domestic /dəˈmestɪk/ adj. 国内的
tack /tæk/ v. 附加
waive /weɪv/ v. 放弃;推迟
amenity /əˈmiːnətɪ/ n. 便利设施,物品
exorbitantly /ɪgˈzɔːbɪtəntlɪ/ adv. 过高
restock /ˌriːˈstɒk/ v. 重新进货
gym /dʒɪm/ n. 健身房
accommodate /əˈkɒmədeɪt/ v. 提供住宿
grill /grɪl/ v. 拷问

A Watch the video twice, and decide whether the following statements are true or false according to the video.

1. _____ When you book your hotel, you do not know some hidden fees. For example, many hotels charge an occupancy tax.
2. _____ Resort fees are your regular room fees, and they also include the fees of the gym, the spa, the pool, etc.
3. _____ A hotel won't waive the fees if you don't ask. And it makes customers unhappy and surprised.
4. _____ If you want to book a hotel, you had better ask the details about the fees.
5. _____ There's usually one service book on the hotel desk, and it will indicate whether there is a fee generally associated with that.

B Watch the video again, and answer the following questions.

1. What kind of hidden fees are commonly found on hotel bills?
   _____.

2. What does "resort fee" include? And how is it calculated in guests' bill?
   _____.

3. What could you do to avoid the fees?
   _____.

4. What could you do to make sure you don't pay the hidden fees when you book a hotel room?
   _____.

5. What is the attitude of the hotel if you don't use the services?
   _____.

Part Four   Dialogues in the Hotel
四、酒店对话

Scenario 1

Take Down Reservations 记录预订

A Listen to the dialogue carefully, and complete the following conversation with what you hear.

Reservationist(R): OK, Mr. Appleton, let me just confirm the details of your reservation. You have reserved (1) _____ at $297 a night for six nights from Friday 21st May. The reservation is made under you, Mr. Jason Appleton. This price includes (2) _____. However 15% of tax on top of the price is excluded. Your contact number is 632-753-255. Is everything correct?

Jason Appleton(J): Yes, that's correct.

R: The reservation is made for you, Mr. Appleton, there's one more thing I'd like to ask. And it's very important to suggest you (3) _____, since May is one of the (4) _____ we receive many reservations each day. If you can guarantee your booking we can make sure the room is guaranteed for you even if you arrived late during night.

J: OK, how do I guarantee my booking?

R: Mr. Appleton, there are usually (5) _____ to do that, you can pay one night's amount in cash to the hotel prior to your arrival, or you could send us a cheque, or the easiest way is to leave your (6) _____ details now.

J: I'll give you my credit card details.

R: Very well Mr. Appleton, I'm ready now.

J: It's 7123-065-077-4376, American Express, and (7) _____ is June 2015.

R: Fantastic. Mr. Appleton, I've guaranteed your booking, your (8) _____ is 657 560 346. I'll send the confirmation email to your address in our system, just to (9) _____. Is it still J.Appleton@cheerful.com?

J: Yes, it's correct.

R: Is there anything else that I can (10) _____?

J: Nothing I can think of right now. Thank you!

R: Thank you for calling Hyatt Regency San Francisco.

B Divide your class into groups of two or three students, and do the dialogue again.

Scenario 2

Keep Updates 保持更新

A Listen to the dialogue carefully and write numbers in the blanks to show the correct order of the conversation.

_____ **Jason (J):** I need to add one more room to my reservation.

_____ **J:** I'd like to change a reservation.

_____ **Receptionist (R):** How would you like to amend your reservation, Mr. Appleton?

_____ **J:** No, I want a standard twin for this one.

_____ **R:** For both rooms?

_____ **R:** Anything else?

_____ **J:** Yes, we're planning to visit Alcatraz for the last 2 days.

_____ **R:** Room Reservations. May I help you, sir?

_____ **R:** In whose name was the reservation?

_____ **J:** Jason Appleton.

_____ **R:** The same room type as your first booking?

_____ **J:** I need to change my booking to 4 nights instead of 6.

_____ **R:** Wonderful. It's all done for you.

B Role play: One student plays the role of receptionist while another plays the role of Jason.

Scenario 3

Ask for a Discount 要求折扣

A Listen to Dialogue 3 and fill in the table with correct information.

Name of guest	Length of the stay	Price of the room	Room preference	Discount (Yes) or (No)

B Listen to the dialogue again, and do a situational dialogue with your partner.

Front Desk(F): Royal Hotel, can I help you?

Jason(J): Yes. I need a room for three nights from May 10 to May 14. Do you have any vacancies?

F: Yes. What kind of room would you like?

J: I'd like a suite with an ocean view, please.

F: No problem, sir.

J: How much will that be?

F: It's 140 dollars per night.

J: That's a bit expensive. I'm told your hotel is offering a discount now.

F: Yes, we were, but the offer ended yesterday. I'm sorry.

J: Oh, I see. Then, do you have anything less expensive?

F: No, sir. This is the least expensive suite we have at the moment.

J: Eh, eh. Let me see. I will book the room.

F: Thank you. Could I have your name, please?

J: My name is Jason Deep.

F: Would you kindly spell that for me?

J: That is J-a-s-o-n D-e-e-p.

F: OK, may I know your cell phone number?

J: It's 18980917378.

F: Thank you. How long would you like to stay?

J: Three nights, from May 10.

F: Certainly, sir. Our check-in time is after 1:00 pm. We look forward to meeting you.

J: Thank you.

Scenario 4

Make a Business Reservation 商务预订

A Listen to Dialogue 4 and mark True or False for the following sentences.

1. _____ It just takes half an hour to travel by car from the airport to the hotel.
2. _____ There is a conference hall that seats four hundred persons in the hotel, and eight meeting rooms which seat twenty persons.
3. _____ The business center of the hotel can provide secretarial and translation services.
4. _____ Single rooms are 720 RMB per day while double rooms are only 880 RMB.
5. _____ After she got information about the hotel, Rosie booked the room at once.

B Listen to the dialogue and answer the following questions:

1. Where is the call from?

2. How many seats are there in the conference room?

3. What services does the business center provide?

4. What are the prices of single rooms and double rooms?

Front Desk(F): Chengdu Hotel, what can I do for you?
Rosie(R): I'm calling from the UK. I want some information before making a reservation.
F: Yes, madam. How can I help you?
R: Firstly, I want to know how far the hotel is from the airport.
F: Only fifty minutes' drive. We have a conference hall that seats four hundred persons. We also have eight meeting rooms which seat twenty persons each.
R: So you must have a business hall.
F: Yes, madam. The business center offers many services. We can provide secretarial and translation services and we of course have fax and telex.
R: What do you charge for double and single rooms?
F: Single rooms are 720 RMB per day while double rooms are only 880 RMB.
R: That sounds very reasonable. Well, I'll have to talk to my boss before making reservations.
F: Do you need any further information, madam?
R: No.
F: Thank you for your calling.

Additional Exercises:

Divide the class into groups. Each group makes a situational dialogue using words or phrases about the hotel reservation. You may refer to the working procedures or sentence patterns in Dialogue 1, Dialogue 2, Dialogue 3 and Dialogue 4.

Additional Words and Phrases 更多的词汇短语储备

Word Tips	
Superior suite 高级套房	Deluxe suite 豪华套房
Executive suite 行政套房	Standard room 标准间
Presidential suite 总统套房	King bed 特大号床
Business suite 商务套房	Atrium-view room 内景房

Part Five Consolidation
五、巩固练习

 Match the terms in column A with the definitions in column B.

A	B
1. amendment	A. guest with reservation did not show up without any notice
2. cancellation	B. a reservation has been confirmed and advanced payment of certain amount made
3. confirmed reservation	C. a company has agreed with the hotel to pay for an agreed number of rooms regardless of whether or not they are used
4. overbooking	D. makes changes to original booking
5. no show	E. a guest arrives at the hotel without a reservation
6. guaranteed reservation	F. guest with reservation informs the hotel or relevant party of foreseeable absence
7. walk-in guest	G. makes more reservation than actual inventory
8. contractual agreement	H. a reservation has been confirmed with guest in writing or verbally

Translation

i. Translate the following sentences into Chinese.
1. I want to reserve a single room (单间) which is better located between 4th floor to 7th floor.
2. A double room with a front view is 140 dollars per night, one with a rear (背面) view is 115 dollars per night.
3. You can cancel (取消) your reservation through hotel website as well as by calling the hotel reservation centre.
4. A reservation has been confirmed and you should make advance payment (预付) of a certain amount.
5. Travelers depend on a well-organized reservation system that is easily accessible through toll-free (免费的) numbers and the Internet.

ii. Translate the following sentences into English.
1. 对不起，没有以您名字预订房间的记录(record)。请问是谁预订的房间？
2. 您也要密切关注网上对该酒店的描述(description)，否则你会觉得上当受骗了。
3. 一百元一天，包括供暖费，但不包括服务费(service charge)。
4. 这款软件可以帮助顾客提前知道房间的入住情况和预订状态(booking status)。
5. 已作担保的预订，如当天取消或没入住(no show)，本酒店将会收取一天的房费。

C Writing

Hotel Reservation Form 酒店预订表

To be a Receptionist or a Concierge, your work may involve making reservations of different kinds. Room reservation or reservations for air tickets and train tickets are usually made by telephone. Usually, the guests send an email to the hotel to get their reservations confirmed. Sometimes, hotel rooms are reserved by sending letters or forms of reservation. To make hotel reservations, the following details must be provided:

(1) Name(s) of guest(s), making sure of the correct spelling.

(2) Date and time of arrival (with request to protect for late arrival. If a shuttle bus or limousine is required, please state it in your letter).

(3) Type of accommodation required.

(4) Date and time of departure.

(5) Method of payment.

(6) Request confirmation on the address the guest provides.

Complete the following hotel reservation form and forward it to Beijing Holiday Inn by email.

Outline:

1. Name of the guest: Song Yaoxian
2. Gender of the guest: Male
3. Date of arrival: January 25th, 2020
4. Date of departure: January 29th, 2020
5. Type of accommodation: Single room with bath
6. Method of payment: Credit card
7. Pick-up service: Limousine

Hotel Reservation

Beijing Holiday Inn
Tel: (010) 62757588 Fax: (010) 62757589

To request a reservation at Beijing Holiday Inn, please complete this form. Group reservations are requested to complete basic information only and type in the comment box particulars of your group.

```
Arrival: Date _____ Month _____ Year _____
Departure: Date _____ Month _____ Year _____
No. of rooms requested: _____ Arrival Flight No.: _____
```

| Room Requests: _____ |
| _____ |

First Name: _____ Family Name: _____
(For a group, please attach a name list)
Telephone: _____ Fax: _____
E-mail: _____
Transportation Shuttle Bus   ○ Yes   ○ No   RMB140 per person per trip
                Limousine   ○ Yes   ○ No   RMB530 per car per trip
Payment to be made on arrival by: ○ Credit Card ○ Cash
Late Arrival Protection: ○ Yes   ○ No

Cancellation will only be accepted in writing with at least 24 hours advance notice prior to the arrival (local time) if reservation is on guarantee.

For late cancellation and guest not showing up on schedule, one night room rental will be debited if reservation is guaranteed by credit card, or one night room rental will be forfeited if advance deposit received.

Confirmation: ○ Yes   ○ No
Comment/Special request:

Signature:

Chapter 2
Registration
入住登记

Major Topics　一、酒店知识：Self Check-in Kiosk 自助登记入住系统
　　　　　　　二、酒店员工：Reception Manager 接待经理
　　　　　　　　　　　　　Reception Supervisor 接待主管
　　　　　　　　　　　　　Shift Leader 值班主管
　　　　　　　　　　　　　Receptionist 接待员
　　　　　　　三、酒店视频：Welcome to Transnational Hotel 欢迎入住跨国酒店
　　　　　　　四、酒店对话：Scenario 1: Registration Requirement 登记须知
　　　　　　　　　　　　　Scenario 2: Group Check-in 团体入住登记
　　　　　　　　　　　　　Scenario 3: Registration Card 入住登记卡
　　　　　　　　　　　　　Scenario 4: Method of Payment 支付方式
　　　　　　　五、巩固练习

　　This chapter concentrates on the topic of registration at Front Desk. In *Part One*, you'll read ABC about Self Check-in Kiosk as a warming-up exercise. In *Part Two*, job description of working staff is provided for you to have some basics about the responsibility of each job in the department. In *Part Three*, you'll watch a short video about how to register at a hotel. In the next section, *Part Four* will provide situational dialogues for you to practice the skills you have learnt about registration based on different scenarios in the hotel. *Part Five* includes some additional exercises to enhance your knowledge and skills of the registration task.

Part One ABC for Hotel
一、酒店知识

Self Check-in Kiosk 自助登记入住系统

Word Tips

innovation /ˌɪnəˈveɪʃn/ n. 创新
modify /ˈmɒdɪfaɪ/ v. 修改
automatically /ˌɔːtəˈmætɪklɪ/ adv. 自动地
interact /ˌɪntərˈækt/ v. 相互影响
multiple /ˈmʌltɪpl/ adj. 多样的
alternative /ɔːlˈtɜːnətɪv/ adj. 可选择的

fantastic /fænˈtæstɪk/ adj. 不可思议的
insert /ɪnˈsɜːt/ v. 插入
redesign /ˌriːdɪˈzaɪn/ v. 重新设计
estate /ɪˈsteɪt/ n. 房地产
boost /buːst/ v. 助推;促进

New modern technology brings numerous innovations to all fields, including accommodation and hospitality. One fantastic innovation is Self Check-in Kiosk deployed in hotels.

Self Check-in Kiosk provides you with fast, convenient and efficient service. Both the hotel and you greatly benefit from this self-service system. Thanks to this intelligently designed and easy-to-interface system, hotel has effective management of personnel and other resources at their property. For you, this system presents an image of friendly, fast and efficient service. The check-in procedure is very simple. What you need to do is to insert your valid credit card, then follow the on-screen instructions. You can locate and modify reservations, print room keys, view and print messages and receive basic information on hotel services via the kiosks. With this machine, you are very easy to locate amenities around a hotel property, such as identifying the best route to a guest room, pool, hotel restaurant or other services. Kiosks can accommodate and serve different language speakers in different languages. Once you leave the hotel, you will automatically be charged.

Hyatt Hotels and Resorts is among the first premier hotel chains to deploy the new and advanced kiosk system as part of its overall lobby redesign moving forward. Integrated into the registration counter, the kiosks have made an immediate impact on customer satisfaction.

A recent study conducted for NCR by Buzzback Market Research revealed that 86 percent of U.S. and Canadian consumers are more likely to do business with a company that offers the flexibility to interact using self-service. The major benefits of Kiosks are: 1) reduction in staff and real estate requirements since one employee can monitor multiple Self-Service Kiosks; 2) unattended operation with extended service hours and off-site locations; 3) providing users with a more enjoyable experience boosting customer satisfaction; 4) tracking usage statistics.

No wonder that more and more hotels and resorts are installing Kiosks as an alternative check-in method.

Based on the above passage, decide whether the following statements are true or false. Write T for true and F for false.

1. _____ One fantastic innovation brought by new modern technology to hotel is Self Check-in Kiosk.
2. _____ This efficient self-service system brings great benefit to guests, but not to hotels.
3. _____ With this machine, you are very easy to locate amenities around a hotel property.
4. _____ Hyatt Hotels and Resorts is the first premier hotel chain to deploy the new and advanced kiosk system.
5. _____ Since Kiosks can bring lots of benefit, more and more hotels and resorts are installing Kiosks.

Part Two　Working Staff
二、酒店员工

1 Listen to the job description of each one in the department, correct the mistakes and put the right ones in the blanks.

(1) **Reception Manager** reports to Front Office Manager. The responsibilities are:

　　To provide a supervisory management function to the Reception.
　　To work closely with Reservation Manager to maximize house occupancy.
　　To ensure that an efficient and professional manner is maintained.
　　To meet targets set for sales and customer satisfaction.
　　　a. _____
　　　b. _____
　　中文提示：
　　　接待经理：向前厅经理汇报，监督管理接待处的工作；密切配合预订经理，争取获得最多的客房收益；确保接待工作专业有效运行；完成预定销售目标以及与客人沟通。

(2) **Reception Supervisor** reports to Reception Manager, makes sure the operations run smoothly. The responsibilities are:

　　To supervise Front Desk operations during shift to a consistently high level.
　　To monitor the standards and performance of team members with an emphasis on training and team work.
　　To deal with guest queries and complaints promptly and efficiently.
　　　a. _____

b. _____

中文提示：

接待主管： 向接待经理汇报，确保接待工作正常运行；监督接待处换班工作，保证其服务水平达到相当高的标准；着重搞好员工培训，强调团队精神，考核工作绩效；回答客人的咨询，快速有效处理投诉。

(3) **Shift Leader** reports to Reception Supervisor, deals with problems in each shift. The responsibilities are:

To monitor the operations for guest arrivals and departures and ensure the smooth running of the daily operations at Reception during shift.

To handle any customer complaints and provide a prompt solution.

To co-ordinate the allocation of bedrooms with the Housekeeping Department.

To organize a shift handover.

a. _____

b. _____

中文提示：

值班主管： 向接待主管汇报，处理倒班期间出现的各种问题，其主要职责有：监督倒班时客人入住、退房工作，保证接待处日常工作正常运行；解决客人投诉，迅速为客人提供解决方案；与客房部协调分房；交接班时做好交接工作。

(4) **Receptionist** provides reception service to every guest. The responsibilities are:

To be ready to provide service for guest registration and departure.

To settle guest accounts, and ensure the bell ringing.

To maintain accurate guest accounts.

To answer and handle queries in a professional and protocol way.

a. _____

b. _____

中文提示：

接待员： 为每一位客人提供服务，主要职责有：随时准备接待客人，登记入住，完善离店手续；为客人结账，结账无误；确保准确的客人登记记录；专业、有礼地回答处理客人的问题。

2 Listen again and discuss the job description of the post you wish to hold in your career.

Part Three Video for the Hotel
三、酒店视频

Welcome to Transnational Hotel 欢迎入住跨国酒店

Word Tips

glitch /glɪtʃ/ n. 过失
jacuzzi /dʒəˈkuːzɪ/ n. 按摩浴缸
valet /ˈvæleɪ/ n. 泊车员
sightseeing /ˈsaɪtsiːɪŋ/ n. 观光
corridor /ˈkɒrɪdɔː(r)/ n. 走廊

adjoined /əˈdʒɔɪnd/ adj. 毗邻的
indoor /ˈɪndɔː(r)/ adj. 室内的
smooth /smuːð/ adj. 顺利的
elevator /ˈelɪveɪtə(r)/ n. 电梯
bellboy /ˈbelbɔɪ/ n. 侍者

A Watch the video twice, and decide whether the following statements are true or false according to the video.

1. _____ Tom Sanders had a reservation with the Transnational Hotel, but the receptionist could not find a record.
2. _____ Tom Sanders did not pay a deposit for his first night, so the hotel cancelled his reservation.
3. _____ The hotel didn't have any more single rooms available, with the exception of one adjoined room which was next to a room where the teenagers live.
4. _____ Tom Sanders needed to pay the extra charge for upgrading his room.
5. _____ The room that Tom Sanders would check in was Room 653 on the 6th floor at the end of the corridor.

B Watch the video again, and answer the following questions.

1. How did Mr. Sanders book with the Transnational Hotel?

2. What were the reasons the receptionist did not allocate Mr. Sanders in a single room?

3. What type of room did Mr. Sanders get eventually?

4. What did the receptionist do to help Mr. Sanders with wireless internet?

5. Did the hotel staff help with Mr. Sanders parking his car? And why?

6. What kind of ID did Mr. Sanders use at registration?
   _____.

7. What did the receptionist mean by "Big Apple"?
   _____.

8. What would Mr. Sanders do in the following days?
   _____.

9. Which room did Mr. Sanders check in?
   _____.

Part Four   Dialogues in the Hotel
四、酒店对话

Scenario 1

Registration Requirement 登记须知

A Listen to Dialogue 1 and mark True or False for the following sentences.

1. _____ Jason White forgot to register his nationality when he checked in.
2. _____ The guest was an American citizen because he was from New York.
3. _____ He had made a reservation for a double room for three nights.
4. _____ He would be leaving the hotel on the 9th after three days.
5. _____ After he printed his card, the clerk told Jason White that his room was Room 862 on the 7th Floor.

B Listen to the dialogue again, and write down the sequence of registration.

1. _____
2. _____
3. _____
4. _____
5. _____
6. _____
7. _____
8. _____
9. _____
10. _____

Clerk(C): Good afternoon. Welcome to Swisstouches Hotel, Xi'an. What can I do for you, sir?

Jason(J): Yes. I'd like to check in, please.

C: Certainly, sir. May I have your name, please?

J: Yes, it's Jason Deep.

C: Would you please complete this registration?

J: Ok, is that right?

C: Um, could you please put your nationality there?

J: Oh, sorry. I forgot it.

C: It doesn't matter. Are you from New York? May I have a look at your passport, please?

J: Yes, of course.

C: OK, thanks. Do you have a reservation with us, sir?

J: Yes, for three nights.

C: Just a moment, please. I'll check our reservation record…Thank you for waiting, sir. Your reservation is for a single room for three nights.

J: Sure.

C: May I confirm your departure time?

J: Yes, I will be leaving on the 8th.

C: How would you like to make payment?

J: By Visa Card.

C: May I take a print of the card, please? Thank you, sir. Your room is 862 on the 8th Floor. Just a moment please. A bellman will show you to your room. I hope you will enjoy your stay with us.

J: Sure. Thank you.

Scenario 2

> **Group Check-in** 团体入住登记

A Listen to Dialogue 2 and fill in the table with correct information.

Categories of check-in	Number of guests	Number of reserved rooms	Documents needed for registration	Person handling registration for the tour group

B Listen to the dialogue again, and do a situational dialogue with your partner.

Guest(G): Excuse me. I am the tour guide of 30 guests. We have booked 16 rooms for tonight. Could you arrange group check-in for us?

Receptionist(R): Certainly, sir. We have the group check-in list ready for you. All I need now is to have 16 guest passports for registration, one for each room.

G: No problem.

R: Excellent! Now, please have the passport holders to sign on the group check-in list. And we'll then give you all the room keys.

G: Thank you very much.

R: You're welcome. I hope you'll enjoy your stay with us.

Scenario 3

Registration Card 入住登记卡

A Listen to Dialogue 3 and write numbers in the blanks to show the correct order of the conversation.

_____ **Clerk (C):** OK, sir. I will need to ask you a couple of questions.

_____ **C:** It's my pleasure. Enjoy your stay!

_____ **C:** May I have your passport number please, Mr. Louis.

_____ **Jason (J):** Yes.

_____ **J:** Sure, it's 65980337993.

_____ **C:** May I have your home address please?

_____ **J:** Thank you. Where is the breakfast served in the morning?

_____ **J:** It's 43 White Glove Road, 11206 NY.

_____ **J:** Thanks a lot.

_____ **C:** Breakfast is served on the 7th floor from 7:50 am to 10:30 am.

_____ **C:** Thank you Mr. Louis. Your room number is 517 on the 5th floor.

_____ **C:** I've enclosed 2 breakfast vouchers in your key holder for you.

_____ **J:** Excellent.

B Role play: One student plays the role of clerk while another plays the role of Jason.

Scenario 4

Method of Payment 支付方式

A Listen to Dialogue 4, and complete the following conversation with what you hear.

Jason (J): Good morning. What is the room rate today?

Clerk (C): It is $190, including (1)_____.

J: I'd like to stay for 4 nights. I'll attend a seminar in the hotel. It is supposed to be held tomorrow morning.

C: Yes, sir. You are welcome to our hotel. Do not hesitate to contact us if you need any help. We are ready to offer you (2)_____.

J: But my credit card is somehow not working today, can I pay (3)_____?

C: Certainly, sir.

J: Good, how much do I have to pay right now?

C: I need the total amount of your 4 days' room charge plus (4)_____ which allows you to use other hotel services in the next 4 days. The room charge for 4 days will be (5)_____

J: That sounds reasonable. Thank you, sir.

C: You are welcome.

B Divide your class into groups of two or three students, and do the dialogue again.

Additional Exercises:

Divide the class into groups. Each group makes a situational dialogue using words or phrases for check-in. You may refer to the working procedures or sentence patterns in Dialogue 1, Dialogue 2, Dialogue 3 and Dialogue 4.

Additional Words and Phrases 更多的词汇短语储备

Word Tips	
information desk 问讯台	registration form 登记表
hotel register 旅客登记簿	questionnaire 意见征询表
hotel card 酒店名片	hotel direction 酒店指南

Chapter 2　Registration 入住登记

Part Five Consolidation
五、巩固练习

 Pair Work: Make up situational dialogues according to the information given below.

	Guest	Hotel Staff
1	request room with a view of pool	arrange the required room; help the guest to complete the registration form; ask for ID
2	request a smoking room, but doesn't like high floors	inform guest all smoking rooms are located on the top floor
3	a tour guide requests a group check-in for 30 people	ask for one passport for each room, and have all the passport holders to sign on the group check-in list
4	ask for bell service and remind the bellman to handle with care	appoint a bellman for the guest
5	call the reception and complain about the air-conditioner	answer the phone and send an engineer upstairs to fix, promise to change room if it can't be fixed

B Translation

i. Translate the following sentences into Chinese.

1. As a hotel policy, we require one day's room charge as a deposit (押金) for guests without reservation.
2. No additional charge is required for children under 12 sharing parents' room without extra (额外的) bed.
3. Half-day room rate (半天房费) will be charged if you check out after 12:00.
4. Could you please put your key on the Reception Counter (前台) when you are out for the sake of safety?
5. This is the receipt, key and the room card (房卡) to Room 1215. The bellman will show you up with your baggage.

ii. Translate the following sentences into English.

1. 先生，您预订的是一个单人间，住两晚。请您填写登记表(registration form)，好吗？
2. 也许是预订系统出现故障(glitch)了。计算机显示您没有预订。
3. 房子整理好前，不管你是在酒店等还是出去走走，最好把行李寄存(store)在前台。
4. 你要做的便是插入(insert)你的有效信用卡，遵照屏幕上提示的操作(on-screen instructions)便可。
5. 请您一定保存好收据(receipt)，否则您离开时将取不回押金(deposit)。

 Writing

Hotel Registration Card 酒店入住登记卡

Whether a hotel is booked through an online travel provider, a travel agent or directly with hotel staff, understanding the details of hotel registration will help ensure you a pleasant stay. Any incorrect information listed on the hotel registration may affect service quality of the hotel as well as your experience when you stay in the hotel.

Suppose you are the guest, fill out the registration card of Holiday Inn Crowne Plaza and deliver it to the Front Desk clerk.

Outline:
1. Name of the guest
2. Gender
3. Nationality
4. Passport number
5. Private address
6. Others

Chapter 3
Concierge
礼宾服务

Major Topics
一、酒店知识：What Is Concierge? 什么是礼宾员？
二、酒店员工：Concierge 礼宾员
　　　　　　　Doorman/Doorkeeper 门童
　　　　　　　Bellman/Porter 行李员
三、酒店视频：Concierge of InterContinental Times Square Hotel 洲际时代酒店的礼宾服务
四、酒店对话：Scenario 1: Bell Service 应接服务
　　　　　　　Scenario 2: Introduction of Room Facilities 介绍房间设施
　　　　　　　Scenario 3: Baggage Deposit 寄存行李
　　　　　　　Scenario 4: Tourism Information 旅游咨询
五、巩固练习

> This chapter concentrates on Concierge. In *Part One*, you'll read ABC about the concierge. In *Part Two*, background knowledge of working staff is provided for you to have some basics about the responsibility of each job for the concierge. In *Part Three*, you'll watch a short video about the concierge of Times Square Hotel. In the next section, *Part Four* will provide some situational dialogues for you to practice the skills you have learnt about the concierge based on different scenarios in the hotel. *Part Five* includes some additional exercises to enhance your knowledge and skills of the concierge.

Part One ABC for Hotel
一、酒店知识

What Is Concierge? 什么是礼宾员?

Word Tips

corporate /ˈkɔːpərət/ adj. 公司的,法人的
prefer /prɪˈfɜː(r)/ v. 优先
amicable /ˈæmɪkəbl/ adj. 友好的;友善的
outlandish /aʊtˈlændɪʃ/ adj. 古怪的;奇异的
prompt /prɒmpt/ adj. 迅速的
confidentiality /ˌkɒnfɪˌdenʃiˈæləti/ n. 机密,机密性

vital /ˈvaɪtl/ adj. 至关重要的
essential /ɪˈsenʃl/ adj. 基本的;必要的
memorable /ˈmemərəbl/ adj. 值得纪念的
demeanor /dɪˈmiːnə/ n. 姿态,气质

What is Concierge? The best way to describe concierge is through an example. Have you noticed a concierge desk at the hotel answering and arranging all that is required by the guest? They help the guest to arrange tour, find out and book restaurants in town or arrange a corporate meeting place.

The word concierge is French in origin and means "keeper of the keys," and as the "keeper," the concierge becomes the point of contact for hotel guests who seek information or assistance during their stay. The hotel concierge position plays a vital role in the daily customer service operations of hotels and resorts.

A hotel concierge position requires a passion for and an understanding of travel and the travel industry. While a degree in hospitality or other related field is often preferred and sometimes required, an in-depth knowledge of the hotel's local area is essential. The concierge position is often demanding and fast-paced, requiring excellent time management and problem-solving skills. On a daily basis the concierge will interact with guests from varied backgrounds and walks of life, and therefore an amicable personality is a must for a successful concierge—fluency in one or more foreign languages is also a plus.

Working as a hotel concierge means that your focus is to ensure that the needs and requests of hotel guests are met, and that each guest has a memorable stay. The hotel concierge is expected to be an expert on his local area. Guests will approach the concierge with questions, seeking suggestions, and demanding problem resolutions. Often concierges will make reservations for restaurants, spas, shows and special events. Requests from guests can range from arranging transportation or providing directions to even the most outlandish seemingly impossible outing. The concierge must make an effort to develop relationships with local business owners and VIPs in order to facilitate the fulfillment of her guests' requests.

Often the concierge becomes the face of the hotel for many guests, which means that appearance and demeanor are of utmost importance. The concierge desk acts as the hub for guest activity planning, which means that the guests' hotel experience depends on the concierge's knowledge and prompt attention. Many business and VIP travelers depend heavily on the concierge, making the position respected and highly regarded.

Don't assume that the job description for a hotel concierge is set in stone, as a concierge receives a vast array of requests and is expected to make even the impossible and unusual happen. While it may seem that the concierge would be a great source for gossip, the opposite is true as the concierge is expected to maintain confidentiality.

The concierge is not a front desk agent and does not take hotel reservations. In some cases the concierge is responsible for managing a section of the hotel's front end staff, so contrary to popular observation the concierge does not work alone.

Based on the above passage, decide whether the following statements are true or false. Write T for true and F for false.

1. _____ The word concierge is French in origin and means "keeper of the keys," whose main obligation is to open the door for the guests who stay in the hotel.
2. _____ The concierge contacts guests from varied backgrounds and walks of life, and therefore a good command of foreign language is a must.
3. _____ The concierge should be a local expert who knows a lot about the local area and also should develop relationships with local business owners.
4. _____ The concierge is the face of the hotel, which means that they must be well dressed and handsome.
5. _____ Although the concierge is a great source for gossip, they keep secrets for guests who stay in the hotel.

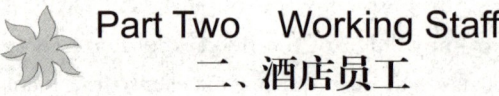

Part Two Working Staff
二、酒店员工

1 Listen to the job description of each one in the department, correct the mistakes and put the right ones in the blanks.

(1) **Concierge** may be involved in maintaining guest records and attending to customer's needs and questions about available facilities and services, travel roads, tours, schedules for outings or transportation as well as making bookings and obtaining tickets for special things.

   a. _____
   b. _____

中文提示：

　　礼宾员：保存客人资料，解答客人对设施、服务、旅游路线、旅游团、外出安排、交通等问题，并帮助客人预订、获取重要节事或活动的门票。

(2) **Doorman/Doorkeeper** creates a friendly atmosphere for hotel guests and facilitate their arrival or departure, including opening doors, picking caps, greeting guests.

　　a. _____
　　b. _____

中文提示：

　　门童：为酒店客人创造欢迎的氛围，并在抵店和离店的时候帮助他们，包括开门、叫出租车、问候客人。

(3) **Bellman/Porter**'s daily tasks: checking whether keys are ready, carrying up luggage, demonstrating the guests how to use the ventilation, television, lights and so on; delivering food, drink and newspapers to customers' rooms, as well as running down, for example picking up dry-cleaning, sending messages and going to post office. In some hotels these jobs are done by doormen.

　　a. _____
　　b. _____

中文提示：

　　行李员：每日工作任务是检查钥匙、搬运行李、向客人展示通风设备、电视机、灯等房间设施的使用方法；送食品、饮料和报纸到客人房间，并完成其他工作，如取干洗衣物、传递信息及邮寄物品。在某些酒店，这些工作由门童完成。

2 Listen again and discuss the job description of the post you wish to hold in your career.

Part Three　Video for the Hotel
三、酒店视频

Concierge of InterContinental Times Square Hotel 洲际时代酒店的礼宾服务

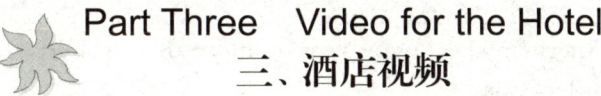

Word Tips
maximize /ˈmæksɪmaɪz/ v. 最大化　　statue /ˈstætʃuː/ n. 雕像
favorite /ˈfeɪvərɪt/ adj. 喜欢的，中意的　　island /ˈaɪlənd/ n. 岛

vintage /ˈvɪntɪdʒ/ n. （葡萄酒）年份 skyscraper /ˈskaɪskreɪpə(r)/ n. 摩天楼
lobby /ˈlɒbɪ/ n. 大厅 lounge /laundʒ/ n. 休息室

A Watch the video twice, and decide whether the following statements are true or false according to the video.

_____ 1. The hotel is located at the Times Square New York.
_____ 2. Sonia is one of the concierge staff at the InterContinental Times Square.
_____ 3. Guests who stayed in the hotel are mainly here just for weekends.
_____ 4. The hotel concierge could get the Broadway shows tickets at a lower price.
_____ 5. The concierge organizes a day trip to the Statue Liberty, the Empire State Building, the Brooklyn Bridge and the Central Park.
_____ 6. Grimaldi's Pizzeria is recommended when you were visiting the Brooklyn Bridge.
_____ 7. China Town and Little Italy have great department stores to enjoy shopping.
_____ 8. The concierge desk could book any museum ticket for its guests.
_____ 9. After showing guests their wonderful room, the concierge team will help them to organize their tour.
_____ 10. Guests could check in at the concierge desk after they see their room.

B Watch the video again, and answer the following questions.

1. How would you plan your schedule if you were in New York for just one week?
   _____.

2. What are the two of the hottest shows in the major theatres?
   _____.

3. What is one of my favorite things to recommend to people in Brooklyn?
   _____.

4. What does West Village mainly do for the customers?
   _____.

5. If the customers check in the hotel, what attitudes they will have towards the hotel according to Sonia Benavides?
   _____.

Part Four Dialogues in the Hotel
四、酒店对话

Scenario 1

Bell Service 应接服务

A Listen to Dialogue 1, and complete the following conversation with what you hear.

Doorman (D): You've finished check-in?
Joan (J): Yes, we've got the key to the room.
D: Shall I take you (1) _____?
J: Yes, let's go.
D: Follow me please. The elevator is (2)_____. Your room is on the fifth floor.
J: Fifth floor is not too high, and it's good.
D: Absolutely! And your room faces the Market Street.
A: Market Street? Well, it gets very noisy during night, I'm a (3) _____.
D: The windows in the Hyatt Regency are all double glazed. And you would be able to see the better view of the city from Market Street, plus the room gets more sunshine on this side.
J: OK, sounds good. Abby, let's see it for one night, if it doesn't work, we can (4) _____.
A: All right, let's give it a go.
D: Don't worry, if you don't like the room, you can inform the front desk or just let me know, we'll arrange another room for you. Is that OK?
J: It's very kind of you.
D: I believe you'll (5) _____. Here is the room.
J: It's nice, it's so spacious. Look at the fresh flowers, Abby, don't you love them?
A: Yes, it's fantastic. It's not noisy at all. We'll stay here.
D: Are you satisfied with the room? Shall we see (6) _____?
J: No, no, the room is perfect for us. Thank you anyway.
D: You are welcome. And hope you'll enjoy your stay. If you need anything or help, you can just call the front desk or (7) _____.
J: Thank you very much!
D: My pleasure.

B Divide your class into groups of two or three students, and do the dialogue again.

Scenario 2

Introduction to Room Facilities 介绍房间设施

A Listen to Dialogue 2 and tell your desk mate where the guest can find each of the room facilities. Fill in the table with correct information.

Underneath the paper on the desk	Next to the door	Next to the suitcase stand	In the corner of the room	On top of the bedside cabinet

B Listen to the dialogue again, and do a situational dialogue with your partner.

Joan (J): What's the paper on the desk, sir?

Doorman (D): It's a "What's on?" It introduces events, exhibitions and gigs in the city.

J: What's underneath?

D: That's hotel manual and a copy of city map. Hotel manual gives you information about Hyatt Regency, and direction of hotel facilities.

J: Um, I got it. And what's that next to the door?

D: It's a suitcase stand to hold your luggage to a comfortable height.

J: Oh, I see. Then, what's next to the suitcase stand?

D: It's a safe to keep valuables. And next to it, is a kettle for you to boil some hot water in the room.

J: Can you tell me how I can use the safe?

D: You just need to set a code of 3 to 9 numbers, and press set code bottom. When you want to open it, just enter the code you set, it will open.

J: Thank you. What's that in the corner?

D: It's a mini-bar. We have prepared some popular drinks and snacks on a reasonable price in the mini-bar for guest to choose. Here is the mini-bar list.

J: Where can I find room service menu if I want to order something to my room?

D: You can find the room service menu on top of the bedside cabinet.

J: Can I get Wi-Fi in the room?

D: Wireless Fidelity is available in every guest room in the hotel. In case of unstable signal, there is also an internet socket next to the telephone socket, and you just need to borrow an internet cable from house keeper with no extra charge.

Scenario 3

Baggage Deposit 寄存行李

A Listen to Dialogue 3 and mark True or False for the following sentences.
1. _____ The guest had four pieces of luggage and two handbags.
2. _____ In his trunk were a watch, porcelain, a bottle of red wine and something fragile.
3. _____ The clerk asked him to take something fragile out, but the guest refused it.
4. _____ The guest would leave for Hangzhou and would be back three days later.
5. _____ The luggage was red or something. And it was square with a yellow leather string around the handle.

B Listen to the dialogue again and answer the following questions.
1. How many pieces of the luggage were there in the guest's trunk?
   _____.
2. Why did the clerk ask the guest to take out articles in the luggage?
   _____.
3. How long would the guest be away from the hotel and where would he leave for?
   _____.
4. What happened to the guest after he came back?
   _____.
5. How did the guest describe details of his luggage?
   _____.

Clerk(C): Good morning, madam. May I help you?
Guest(G): Yes, I'd like to check my baggage.
C: May I have your name and room number?
G: Yes, here is the card. How many pieces of luggage have you got?
C: I've got four pieces in all.
G: That is right.
C: When will you want it?
G: In three days.
C: Would you like to check your luggage here, sir?
G: Yes, I'm leaving for Hangzhou today and I'll be back in three days. So I'll leave the trunk in the storeroom.
C: Is there any food, anything valuable or breakable in the trunk?
G: Oh, here is a watch, porcelain and a bottle of whiskey.
C: I'm afraid you have to take them out. The whiskey is combustible, the porcelain is a fragile object and the watch is also valuable.
G: I'm sorry. I didn't know. I'll take them out. Is everything OK?

C: Yes, thank you for your cooperation. Have a good journey!
G: Thank you.

(After three days, the guest comes back.)

G: I'll sorry. I've lost my tags. How can I do about it?
C: Would you please show me your key card?
G: Here it is.
C: I see. What is your baggage? And do you remember the tag number or the color of your luggage?
G: Uh, it is red or something. Uh, it is like this. It is square with a leather cover. Yes, I remember, there is green string around the handle. That is right.
C: I will check it for you... sorry for keeping you waiting. I've found it. Is this yours?
G: All right.

Scenario 4

Tourism Information 旅游咨询

A Listen to Dialogue 4 and write numbers in the blanks to show the correct order of the conversation.

_____ **Doorman (D):** It's not far from the hotel, Ma'am. You can walk or take a bus. It depends on how you want to get there.

_____ **Abby (A):** Sounds too much hassle.

_____ **A:** Hi, we want to go to Pier 39. Could you tell us how to get there from the hotel?

_____ **A:** How long it will take to walk there?

_____ **D:** That's true. It's easier just walk or if you like, I could flag a taxi for you.

_____ **D:** Absolutely Ma'am. When you go out of the hotel, on your left-hand side is Market St. Go down Market St to the waterfront, and follow the San Francisco Bay Trail for 25 minutes. Pier 39 is on your right-hand side. You won't miss it.

_____ **D:** If you take a bus, you have to first walk about 5 minutes to Market St & Front St, then, take Bus 38 from there, change to Bus 91 at Kearny St & Geary Blvd, get off at Columbus Ave & North Point St, then walk to Pier 39. Actually walk is the easiest way to get there. It's only about 30 minutes if you walk.

_____ **A:** I think we'll just walk there. Could you tell us the direction?

_____ **A:** Thank you!

_____ **D:** My pleasure.

B Role play: One student plays the role of a doorman while another plays the role of Abby.

Additional Exercises:

Divide the class into groups. Each group makes a situational dialogue using words or phrases for the concierge. You may refer to the working procedures or sentence patterns in Dialogue 1, Dialogue 2, Dialogue 3 and Dialogue 4.

Part Five   Consolidation
五、巩固练习

A Pair Work: Make up situational dialogues according to the information given below.

	Guest	Concierge
1	ask for bell service and an extra bed	inform extra bed is 400 RMB per night
2	ask for a copy of city map	suggest the city map in guest room
3	ask for the location of City Museum	suggest No.5 bus at the bus stop out of the hotel, and get off at Nanjing Road
4	request a baby sitter from 2–6 p.m., ask for an authentic Sichuan restaurant and reserve a table for 2 at 6:30 p.m.	ask for the baby's detail suggest Red Chili restaurant, and ask for preference of table
5	appreciate his/her help, and try to tip 20 RMB	thanks for his/her kindness and take the gratuity

B Translation

i. Translate the following sentences into Chinese.

1. According to the regulation, we don't accept food, combustible (易燃), valuable and breakable objects.
2. When you return to the hotel, please show this hotel card (酒店名片) to the taxi driver.
3. When you check out (离店), please call number 32 and we'll help you with your baggage immediately.
4. Most taxi drivers do not speak English. It is helpful if you have your destination (目的地) written in Chinese.
5. He left a message (便条) for you. There was also a telephone call from a lady. She asked you to ring her up this evening.

ii. Translate the following sentences into English.
1. 当客人办理入住手续时，行李员要把行李放到行李推车上并等候客人完成登记。
2. 您床头的台子装有自动叫醒器(waking device)。我想你不会睡过头的。
3. 如果您希望在房间里用早餐，请通过电话申请客房服务(room service)。
4. 顺便告诉您，我们结账离店(check-out)的时间是中午12点钟。
5. 我们酒店没有接送服务(pick-up service)。我能为您叫一辆出租车吗？

C Writing

Memo writing is practically a requirement in the hotel. Usually, memos allow employees to communicate with others in their organization without having to schedule a meeting. And, unlike letters, there is no need to address each individual in the company.

Suppose you are a desk clerk and will have a work shift, write a memo to your colleague, and remind him/her to pass the message to Jason who will be back to the hotel in the afternoon.

Outline:
1. Mr. White visited Jason at 2:30 p.m., but he was not in the hotel.
2. Jason's cell phone is out of service.
3. A party in honor of Jason and his wife will be postponed at 7:00 p.m. tomorrow.
4. A pick-up service is available. Pick-up time is 6:30 p.m.

Chapter 4
Private Branch Exchange
总　机

Major Topics　　一、酒店知识：IP Private Branch Exchange in Hotels 酒店网络电话总机
　　　　　　　　　二、酒店员工：Private Branch Exchange Manager 总机经理
　　　　　　　　　　　　　　　Private Branch Exchange Supervisor 总机领班
　　　　　　　　　　　　　　　Private Branch Exchange Operator 总机接线员
　　　　　　　　　三、酒店视频：Caller's Experience Training 总机接线员培训
　　　　　　　　　四、酒店对话：Scenario 1: External Calls 外线电话
　　　　　　　　　　　　　　　Scenario 2: Internal Calls 内线电话
　　　　　　　　　　　　　　　Scenario 3: Wake-up Call 叫醒电话
　　　　　　　　　　　　　　　Scenario 4: Collect Call 接听人付费电话
　　　　　　　　　五、巩固练习

　　　This chapter concentrates on the Private Branch Exchange (PBX). In *Part One*, you'll read ABC about the IP PBX as a warming-up exercise. In *Part Two*, job description of working staff is provided for you to have some basics about the responsibility of each job at PBX. In *Part Three*, you'll watch a short video about the phone skills and etiquette you need to know in your hospitality career. In the next section, *Part Four* will provide some situational dialogues for you to practice the PBX service based on different scenarios. *Part Five* includes additional exercises to enhance your knowledge and skills about calling or working in a hotel, and get to know how to receive a call from guests in a proper way.

Part One ABC for Hotel
一、酒店知识

IP Private Branch Exchange in Hotels 酒店网络电话总机

Word Tips

absurdly /əbˈsɜːdlɪ/ adv. 荒谬地
maintain /meɪnˈteɪn/ v. 保持
significantly /sɪgˈnɪfɪkəntli/ adv. 显著地
framework /ˈfreɪmwɜːk/ n. 架构
critical /ˈkrɪtɪkl/ adj. 至关重要的
revenue /ˈrevənjuː/ n. 收入,收益
toll /təʊl/ n. 税;费
unavoidable /ˌʌnəˈvɔɪdəbl/ adj. 不可避免的
application /ˌæplɪˈkeɪʃn/ n. 应用

Some of you may have noticed that hotels used to (or even still) charge you 15%—20% surcharge above telephone charges if you want to call external numbers. Although call charges were absurdly high, the truth is that revenue from such charges can't even cover half of the telecommunication cost in most hotels. As future hoteliers, what can we do to cut down the cost while maintaining guest stay experience? Well, IP PBX can be one prosperous solution.

IP PBX uses internet instead of public switched telephone network as the communication carrier. Hence it avoids huge tolls and charges collected by traditional telecommunication companies. Therefore, the cost can drop significantly.

Meanwhile, be able to enjoy unlimited call access—local, long-distance, even international without adding extra charges on the bill surely can be a plus in majority guests' opinion.

Be aware that majority of calls in a hotel actually are made by hotel staff. Especially in large hotel chains, communication among properties in different locations is essential to smooth operation. However, does that mean high long-distance cost is really unavoidable? The answer is no. Nowadays, IP PBX can solve the problem easily. By using one framework, calls between hotels is just one extension away.

Furthermore, IP PBX which uses broadband internet is easier integrated with other hotel systems, such as Property Management System, etc. Although behind the scenes activities are invisible to guests, they are critical to hotel daily operation.

Of course IP PBX is not perfect—at least yet. The calling quality provided by IP PBX is normally lower than traditional telecommunication companies. And the calls are more easily interrupted. Furthermore, the system is more exposed to common risks on internet such as privacy issues, computer viruses and hacker attacks.

Based on the above passage, decide whether the following statements are true or false. Write T for true and F for false.

1. _____ Hotels usually charge the guests 15%—20% surcharge above telephone charges so they can make a lot of profits.
2. _____ IP PBX can provide services such as connecting local calls, international calls, room calls and extensions as well as sending faxes.
3. _____ Hotels save costs because they do not pay charges collected by traditional telecommunication companies and pay tolls only using IP PBX system.
4. _____ It is costly to integrate an IP PBX system with other applications such as Property Management System, etc.
5. _____ IP PBX is not as perfect as guests expect because the calls are frequently interrupted and hackers often attack the system.

Part Two　Working Staff
二、酒店员工

1 Listen to the job description of each one in the department, correct the mistakes and put the right ones in the blanks.

(1) **Private Branch Exchange Manager,** the head of reception, responsible for PBX operation, reports to Assistant Manager of Lobby.
   a. _____
   b. _____
   中文提示：
   　　总机经理：总机的负责人，负责整个部门的经营管理，向前厅部经理汇报工作。

(2) **Private Branch Exchange Supervisor** assists PBX Manager in daily operation, responsible for the recruiting and performance of PBX staff, reports to Front Office Manager.
   a. _____
   b. _____
   中文提示：
   　　总机领班：协助总机经理进行日常营运，负责总机员工的培训和管理，向总机经理汇报工作。

(3) **Private Branch Exchange Operator,** responsible for answering and transferring external calls, answering general inquiries, providing morning call service and performing other functions of PBX, reports to PBX Supervisor.
   a. _____

b. _____

中文提示：

总机接线员： 负责接听和转接电话，回答一般性提问，提供叫醒服务以及其他总机服务，向总机领班汇报工作。

2 Listen again and discuss the job description of the post you wish to hold in your career.

Part Three Video for the Hotel
三、酒店视频

Caller's Experience Training 总机接线员培训

Word Tips

deliver /dɪˈlɪvə(r)/ v. 传递，传达
interact /ˌɪntərˈækt/ v. 互动，相互作用
cram /kræm/ v. 塞满；猛吃
appreciate /əˈpriːʃieɪt/ v. 感激
defensive /dɪˈfensɪv/ adj. 防御的

promptly /ˈprɒmptli/ adv. 迅速地，立即
succinct /səkˈsɪŋkt/ adj. 简洁的
accidentally /ˌæksɪˈdentəli/ adv. 意外地
interrupt /ˌɪntəˈrʌpt/ v. 打断，打乱
clarification /ˌklærəfɪˈkeɪʃn/ n. 澄清，阐明

A Watch the video twice, and decide whether the following statements are true or false according to the video.

1. _____ The PBX operator should answer the phone within 3 seconds. The sooner, the better.
2. _____ The attitude to the caller is more important than answering the phone promptly.
3. _____ Before picking up the receiver, the operator should stop talking with others, but he or she may do other things.
4. _____ The operator may ask the caller to hold on while providing some on-hold message during his or her wait time.
5. _____ How the operator handles guests' call and their request will make it a great experience for them.

B Watch the video again, and answer the following questions.

1. What is the best time when you answer the caller's phone? Why?

2. What do you need to care when you listen to the caller?
   _____.

3. What should you do before you put a caller on hold?
   _____.

4. What would you do when you are online while the second call comes in?
   _____.

5. Instead of saying "I don't know," what should you say to the caller?
   _____.

Part Four   Dialogues in the Hotel
四、酒店对话

Scenario 1

External Calls 外线电话

A Listen to Dialogue 1, and complete the following conversation with what you hear.

Operator (O): Good afternoon, Shangri-la Hotel. How may I help you?

Mr. Urie (U): I just landed at your city. How can I get to your hotel?

O: Which (1) _____ are you in right now, sir?

U: East End Airport, I believe. Just a minute. Yes, right, I'm in (2)_____.

O: Then you can come to our hotel by (3) _____.

U: I see. No, I can't take bus. I need to visit several places in your city tomorrow. I'd better rent (4)_____ and drive.

O: Well, there is an Avis counter in Arrival Hall.

U: Great. How long does it take to drive to your hotel?

O: It will only take you about (5) _____.

U: Can you tell me how?

O: In this case, do you mind if I transfer you to (6) _____? They can give you detailed direction.

U: OK.

O: *(Call Concierge)* Hi, Jimmy, this is Paula in PBX. There is a gentleman (7) _____. He needs to know how to drive to our hotel. I'll transfer him to you right now.

(Transfer the call)

B Divide your class into groups of two or three students, and do the dialogue again.

Scenario 2

Internal Calls 内线电话

A Listen to Dialogue 2 and mark the following sentences with T(true) or F(false).

1. _____ The guest wonders if it is possible for him to extend the stay in the hotel for two days.
2. _____ It depends on the hotel's booking situation. The guest may remain in his room.
3. _____ The new guest will check in at 9:00 a.m., so Mr. Douglass has to move to another room.
4. _____ The guest is not so happy because he is requested to move to Room 1548.
5. _____ The guest has to carry his own luggage because he is a regular guest in the hotel.

B Listen to the dialogue again and answer the following questions.

1. Why does the guest want to extend his stay in the hotel?
   _____

2. What's the possible way to solve the problem before the new guest checks in?
   _____

3. When will the guest leave next morning?
   _____

4. What is the guest required to do next day? And why?
   _____

Operator (O): Good morning! Can I help you?

Douglass (D): Good morning! I'm calling from Room 1208. My business negotiation has progressed much more slowly than I had expected. This makes it necessary for me to stay on here for another day. I wonder if it is possible for me to extend my stay in your hotel for two days.

O: I'll take a look at the hotel's booking situation. Yes, sir. I'm glad that we'll be able to accept your extension request. But I'm afraid that it will be necessary for us to ask you to change room for the last two nights. You see, we have already let your room to another gentleman. Is that acceptable to you?

D: Yes, that's no problem at all.

O: Let me see... Room 1548 will be vacant. How about Room 1548?

D: That is fine.

O: When would you like to move tomorrow?

D: I don't know.

O: The new occupant will be checking in a little after twelve.

D: That means I have to move out before 12 o'clock. Let me see. I'll be leaving for the negotiation at 9:30 tomorrow morning and I will not be returning to the hotel until sometime in the afternoon. So I'm going to have to do it before I go to the negotiation. Well, I think I'll move at 9 o'clock.

O: Good. I'll send a bellboy to your room and help you with your luggage at 9 o'clock. And please remember to bring your key card to the reception desk when you pass it tomorrow so that I can change the room number on it.

D: I will. Thank you very much.

O: With pleasure.

Scenario 3

Wake-up Call 叫醒电话

A Listen to Dialogue 3 and fill in the table with correct information.

Name of the guest	Gender of the guest	The first time of wake-up call	The second time of wake-up call	Service requested

B Listen to the dialogue again, and do a situational dialogue with your partner.

Operator (O): Good evening, PBX. How may I help you, Mr. Grison?
Mr. Grison (G): I would like to have a wake-up call for tomorrow.
O: Of course. What time would you like it?
G: Five o'clock. My wife and I need to catch plane.
O: Then, would you like a second wake-up call?
G: Sure. Call us again at 5:10 please.
O: (*Record the time*) All set, Mr. Grison. Anything else I can do for you?
G: That's all. Thank you.
O: You are welcome, sir.
G: Bye.
O: Goodbye. Have a nice evening.
(*The next morning at five o'clock.*)
O: Good morning, Mr. & Mrs. Grison. This is your five o'clock wake-up call.
G: Thanks. (*Hang up the phone*)
(*5:10*)
O: Good morning, Mr. & Mrs. Grison. This is your second wake-up call at 5:10.
G: Oh, thank you. By the way, could you connect us to Room Service?
O: Of course, Mr. Grison. I'll transfer you right now. Have a nice day.

Scenario 4

Collect Call 接听人付费电话

A Listen to Dialogue 4 and write down the relevant information you hear.

1. Caller's Name: _____
2. Receiver's Name: _____
3. Room number: _____
4. Place of caller: _____
5. Categories of call: _____
6. Hotel operator number: _____
7. International operator number: _____

International Operator (I): This is Bombay calling. I have a call for Mr. Tom Smith.
Operator (O): Bombay for Mr. Tom Smith. Do you know his room number, please?
I: Yes, it's 3820.
O: Thank you. Is this a paid call?
I: It's collect.
O: May I know who is calling, please?
I: Yes. Pradip Patel.
O: How do you spell that, please?
I: Pakistan P, America A, Tokyo T, England E, London L.
O: Mr. Pradip Patel. Thank you. Just a moment, please.

(Calls Room 3820)

O: May I speak to Mr. Tom Smith, please?
Guest (G): Speaking. What can I do for you?
O: This is the Hotel Operator. I have a collect call from Mr. Pradip Patel in Bombay. Will you accept the charges?
G: Yes, of course.
O: Thank you. Could you hold the line, please?

(Speaks to the international operator)

O: Hello. Mr. Smith will accept the call. Could you give me your operator number, please?
I: Yes, it's 23.
O: Thank you. My number is 54. Could you give me the time and the charges after the call, please?
I: Yes, of course.
O: Thank you. Go ahead, please.

> **Additional Exercises:**

Divide the class into groups. Each group makes a situational dialogue using words or phrases for the PBX. You may refer to the working procedures or sentence patterns in Dialogue 1, Dialogue 2, Dialogue 3 and Dialogue 4.

Part Five   Consolidation
五、巩固练习

A Match the terms in column A with the definitions in column B.

A	B
1. PBX	A. An abbreviation which stands for "24 hours a day, 7 days a week," usually referring to a production line or service facility or any other business available at all times without interruption.
2. extension	B. Any process that has the aim of augmenting knowledge, resolving doubt, or solving a problem.
3. external call	C. A service provided by most lodging establishments to provide a service similar to alarm clocks via a telephone. In UK, it is called alarm call, in Asia, morning call.
4. internal call	D. A telephone exchange that serves a hotel and makes connections among the internal telephones of the property and also connect them to the public switched telephone network (PSTN). It is also referred to the department that use the system and mainly take charge of transferring calls.
5. inquiry	E. Any end point on a private branch exchange system.
6. wake-up call	F. A call made from the same private branch exchange system.
7. 24/7	G. A call made from public switched telephone network.

B Translation

  i. Translate the following sentences into Chinese.
   1. "Please" and "Thank you" will probably be the most frequently used words (最常使用的词汇) at PBX.
   2. Never leak guest's information to an outsider (外人). This is the hotel policy (酒店规定).

3. Mr. Wang is not in Room 1523. Would you like to leave a message on his voice mail (语音信箱), then?
4. There's a bad connection. There may be a fault (故障) on the line.
5. I'm sorry the number is engaged. And it took me quite a long time getting to you.

ii. Translate the following sentences into English.
1. 请问是哪位? 我听不清楚您是谁。您能讲大声点吗?
2. 对不起,他在接另一个电话。您要稍等 (hold)一下吗?
3. 我几乎听不到你在说什么。可能是听筒 (receiver)没放好。
4. 对不起,你说谁? 我不认识这个人。
5. 我想您不会睡过头的。我们会在6:30分提供第二次电话叫醒服务 (wake-up call)。

 Writing

Note 便签

Note writing has always been a special way for people to communicate, and has become even more special in an age of telephones, voice mail and quick e-mails. Taking the time to write and send notes can display good etiquette and courtesy and extra thoughtfulness.

Working in PBX, it is necessary for the operator to take notes lest he might forget important information. Suppose you're the operator of PBX, write a note using beautiful and thoughtful words, and then forward it to the guest who is not in the room of hotel by voice mail.

Outline:
1. The name of guest: Tom Smith
2. Gratitude for his help with the poor students
3. Inviting him to make a presentation at 9:00 a.m. tomorrow
4. Waiting in the lobby at 8:30 a.m.
5. Complimentary remarks

Chapter 5
Check-out
退 房

Major Topics   一、酒店知识：Cashier's Jobs at Reception 前厅接待处收银员的工作
　　　　　　　　二、酒店员工：Reception Manager 接待经理
　　　　　　　　　　　　　　Duty Manager 值班经理
　　　　　　　　　　　　　　Reception Supervisor 前台领班
　　　　　　　　　　　　　　Receptionist 前台接待员
　　　　　　　　三、酒店视频：Check-out Front Desk 前台退房
　　　　　　　　四、酒店对话：Scenario 1: Check Out Group Guests 为团队客人退房
　　　　　　　　　　　　　　Scenario 2: Handle Disputed Charges 处理有争议的账单
　　　　　　　　　　　　　　Scenario 3: Check Out FIT 为散客退房
　　　　　　　　　　　　　　Scenario 4: Foreign Currency Exchange 货币兑换
　　　　　　　　五、巩固练习

　　　　The main topic of this chapter is check-out. In *Part One*, you'll read ABC about cashier's jobs related with the Reception such as check-out. In *Part Two*, job description of working staff is provided for you to have some basics about the responsibility of each job at Front Desk. In *Part Three*, you'll watch a short video about how to handle check-out formalities for guests. In the next section, *Part Four* will provide situational dialogues for you to practice the check-out skills you have learnt based on different scenarios. *Part Five* includes some additional exercises to enhance your knowledge and skills in a hotel, and get to know how to act in a normative way.

Part One ABC for Hotel
一、酒店知识

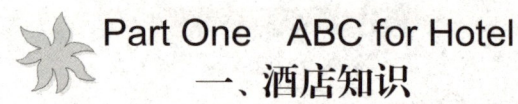

Cashier's Jobs at Reception 前厅接待处收银员的工作

Word Tips

check-out /tʃek aʊt/ n. 退房
refund /ˈriːfʌnd/ v. 退还, 偿还
cheque /tʃek/ n. 支票
petty /ˈpeti/ adj. 小额的, 一点点
audit /ˈɔːdɪt/ v. 审计, 查账
censor /ˈsensə(r)/ n. 检查, 审查

cashier /kæˈʃɪə(r)/ n. 出纳员, 收银员
deposit /dɪˈpɒzɪt/ n. 押金, 保证金
encashment /ɪnˈkæʃmənt/ n. 兑付现款
frequency /ˈfriːkwənsi/ n. 频率; 频繁
simplify /ˈsɪmplɪfaɪ/ v. 简化, 使简单
withdraw /wɪðˈdrɔː/ v. (从银行)取钱

Cashier's jobs related with the Reception such as check-out are handled by cashiers from Finance Department in many Chinese hotels, but in most international hotels these jobs are mainly done by receptionists. Generally speaking, cashier's jobs include refund of cash deposits, giving changes, cash credit cards, cash traveler's cheques, cash paid-outs, exchange currencies etc. Besides refunding cash deposits and giving changes, other services usually come with service charges which are certain percent of the encashment amount.

In order to provide above services, receptionists are assigned with petty cash—certain amount of cash issued by Finance Controller (or Director of Finance). The amount of petty cash varies from hotel to hotel—mainly depends on the frequency of cash usage. Even within the same hotel, the amount varies among different rankings. Supervisor and Reception Manager (and/or Duty Manager) normally hold larger amount. In some hotels, petty cash is assigned to each receptionist, while in the others is assigned to each shift. Either way, the staff holding the petty cash is responsible for the accuracy and safety of this money. Petty cash is to be audited by Finance Department on regular basis.

Thanks to the modern technology, receptionist's cashier works are more and more simplified. For example, advanced mini-bar within built-in censor can automatically post any charges to guest bills. Hence it can save receptionist a lot of time of waiting room-inspection at check-out. Also, in the past, a receptionist might need to perform a lot of currency exchange or traveler's cheque encashment for international guests. Nowadays, the guest will probably go straightly to an ATM nearby and withdraw local currency from his or her credit card.

Based on the above passage, decide whether the following statements are true or false. Write T for true and F for false.

1. _____ Hotel charges guests service fees for refunding cash deposit.
2. _____ In a large hotel where majority of guests rarely use cash, the amount of its receptionist's petty cash is probably small.
3. _____ Receptionist holding the petty cash is responsible for the accuracy and safety of this money.
4. _____ Nowadays, an international guest possessing a credit card is less likely to withdraw local currency from ATM than to obtain cash at Reception.

Part Two Working Staff
二、酒店员工

1 Listen to the job description of each one in the department, correct the mistakes and put the right ones in the blanks.

(1) **Reception Manager:** head of reception, responsible for business operation, reports to Front Office Manager; sometimes he or she is the Administrative Director.
   a. _____
   b. _____
   中文提示：
   　　接待经理：前台负责人，负责前台营运，向前厅部经理汇报，有的时候由前厅部经理兼任。

(2) **Duty Manager** assists Reception Manager in daily operation—mainly faces the guests, for example, meeting VIP, maintaining guest satisfaction, and solving complaints. In some hotels, this post is held by Reception Clerk, who reports to Reception Manager. In the others, this post is the same rank as Reception Manager.
   a. _____
   b. _____
   中文提示：
   　　大堂经理：协助接待经理日常营运，主要负责对客方面，例如接待贵宾、确保客人满意和处理投诉。一些酒店里这个职位由前台领班担任，并向接待经理汇报工作，而另一些酒店里则和接待经理同级。

(3) **Reception Supervisor** assists Reception Manager in shift operation, manages Receptionists, and reports to Duty Manager.
   a. _____
   b. _____

中文提示：

前台领班：协助接待经理日常营运，管理前台员工，向接待经理汇报工作。

(4) **Receptionist** is responsible for check-in and registration, answers general information and offers other services, reports to Reception Supervisor.

   a. _____
   b. _____

中文提示：

前台接待员：负责登记入住和退房，回答一般性提问以及其他前台服务，向前台领班汇报工作。

2 Listen again and discuss the job description of the post you wish to hold in your career.

Part Three　Video for the Hotel
三、酒店视频

Check-Out Front Desk 前台退房

Useful Words and Expressions

suitcase /ˈsuːtkeɪs/ n. 手提箱　　　　　statement /ˈsteɪtmənt/ n. 对账单
charge /tʃɑːdʒ/ n. 收费，要价　　　　connection /kəˈnekʃn/ n. 联系
excessive /ɪkˈsesɪv/ adj. 过分的，过度的　rental /ˈrentl/ adj. 出租的，租赁的
shuttle /ˈʃʌtl/ n. 短程往返巴士　　　　park /pɑːk/ v. 停车，停靠

A Watch the video twice, and decide whether the following statements are true or false according to the video.

1. _____ Mr. Mario called the front desk and asked the bellman to pick up the luggage in Room 513 and 515.
2. _____ Mr. Mario made a phone call to the Front Desk, but never made a connection, so they came to the Reception to check out.
3. _____ There were charges for pay TV, telephone and something from Fitness Center on the bill.

4. _____ Mr. Mario and Mr. Alexander thought the hotel charges were excessive, so they refused to pay.

5. _____ The two guests had someone help with the bags, and headed for the airport by the shuttle bus.

B Watch the video again, and answer the following questions.

1. Where was Mr. Mario's suitcase?
_____.

2. What were the charges on their bill? Why did Mario deny the phone charges?
_____.

3. What time did the airport shuttle leave?
_____.

4. Why did they just move to check out instead of arguing for the disputed charge?
_____.

Part Four Dialogues in the Hotel
四、酒店对话

Scenario 1

Check Out Group Guests 为团队客人退房

A Listen to Dialogue 1, and complete the following conversation with what you hear.

Claire (C): Good morning, Ms. Lane. How are you today?

Ms. Lane (L): Fine, thanks. I'm leaving. Here is the (1) _____.

C: Thank you. Have you (2) _____?

L: Absolutely.

C: Thank you. Am I to understand that your room charge is paid by the conference ledger?

L: That's right. I believe there are only a few incidentals to settle.

C: Seems right. Do you have any (3) _____ such as mini-bar?

L: I don't think so.

C: Great. Then here is your bill. If everything is correct, please (4) _____.

L: (Sign and give it back) Here you are.

C: Would you like me to put these charges on the credit card you gave us?

L: Actually, I shall pay them (5) _____.

C: No problem. (Take the money and give back changes) Here is your change and here is your (6) _____. The shuttle your conference arranged to airport is leaving from the right side of the (7) _____. Need any luggage assistance?

L: Not really. But could you hold my luggage for two minutes? I want to grab a cup of coffee before I go.

C: Of course.

L: Thanks. (*Leaves, then comes back with coffee*) Now I'm ready for my luggage.

C: Here you are, Ms. Lane. Have a safe trip and look forward to (8) _____.

B Divide your class into groups of two or three students, and do the dialogue again.

Scenario 2

Handle Disputed Charges 处理有争议的账单

A Listen to Dialogue 2 and write numbers in the blanks to show the correct order of the conversation.

_____ **Claire (C):** Absolutely. Did you enjoy this stay?

_____ **Mr. Miller (M):** Yes, as usual. Here is the room key.

_____ **M:** Maybe, I was on the phone then. But I don't think it is right for me to pay, because I turned off the movie as soon as I hung up. I didn't even know what it was talking about.

_____ **C:** Good morning, Mr. Miller. You look wonderful today.

_____ **C:** Well ... Then, I have to report to our Duty Manager. Please wait a few minutes.

_____ **C:** Thanks. And here is your bill.

_____ **M:** Thank you, Claire. Can I have my bill, please?

_____ **M:** Let me see. Uh ... I think this is not right. I ordered only one movie on Friday night, not two.

_____ **M:** That's all right.

_____ **C:** Well, I guess that's because the preview is only for 15 minutes and you might forget to click "Quit."

B Role play: One student plays the role of Claire while another plays the role of Mr. Miller.

Scenario 3

> **Check Out FIT 为散客退房**

A Listen to Dialogue 3 and fill in the table with correct information.

Name of guest	Room number	Length of the stay	Total amount of the bill	Hotel policy

B Listen to the dialogue again, and do a situational dialogue with your partner.

Cashier(C): Good morning, sir. May I help you?

Guest (G): I'm leaving today. Can I check out now?

C: Certainly, sir. Would you please tell me your name and room number?

G: James Smith, Room 2143.

C: Thank you, Mr. Smith.

(*Checking the computer*) So you have stayed here for four nights?

G: Yes, exactly.

C: Have you used the mini bar this morning?

G: Yes. I used it. I drank a can of Coca-Cola.

(*Mr. Kang phones the Housekeeping.*)

C: Here's the bill. It totals 3,894 *Yuan*. Please have a check.

G: It's OK.

C: Mr. Smith, you've paid 4,000 *Yuan* as the deposit. So I'll refund you 106 *Yuan*. And here is your invoice.

G: One more thing, I have a business meeting till 2:00 p.m. May I leave my luggage in the room till then?

C: Mr. Smith, as you know, our regular check-out time is 12:00. According to our hotel policy, a half day's rent is charged against a room not vacated after 12:00. But since you are our repeat guest, we can give you a later check-out time. But it should not be later than 2:30 p.m.

G: That's very kind of you.

Scenario 4

| Foreign Currency Exchange 货币兑换 |

A Listen to Dialogue 4 and mark the following sentences with T(true) or F(false).

1. _____ The guest wants to cash his personal checks and change some Euros in the hotel.
2. _____ The hotel accepts cash, credit card, and traveler's checks, as well as personal checks.
3. _____ The guest must present his identity card when he exchanges foreign currencies.
4. _____ The guest is requested to fill in one memo before he exchanges US dollars.
5. _____ The guest needs one-dollar notes because he wants to go shopping in the duty-free shops.

B Listen to the dialogue again and answer the following questions:

1. What was the exchange rate on that day?

2. What should the guest write on the memo for exchanging dollars?

3. What does the cashier remind the guest to do after exchange of the money?

4. What can the guest do with the RMB left with him?

Cashier(C): Good afternoon, sir. Can I help you?

Guest (G): May I cash my personal checks here and I'd like to change some US dollars.

C: I'm afraid not. We accept cash, credit card, and traveler's checks only. I hope it doesn't cause you any inconvenience. But you're welcome to change money here.

G: Well, I'll change three hundred. And...what is today's exchange rate?

C: According to today's exchange rate, every US dollar in cash is equivalent to 6.15 *Yuan*. Would you please fill in this memo and show me your passport?

G: I see.

C: Please write your name, passport number and room number on this slip.

G: Here you are.

C: Thank you. You'll have it right away.

G: OK. Will you please give me some one-*Yuan* notes? I need some small change.

C: All right, sir. (*Changing the money*) Here it is. Please have a check. And keep the exchange memo.

G: Oh, yes, thanks. By the way, can you tell me what I should do with the RMB left with me?

C: You'll have to go to the Bank of China or the airport exchange office to change it back dollars by showing the memo.

G: I see. Thanks.
C: You are welcome.

Additional Exercises:

Divide the class into groups. Each group makes a situational dialogue using words or phrases for the check-out. You may refer to the working procedures or sentence patterns in Dialogue 1, Dialogue 2, Dialogue 3 and Dialogue 4.

Part Five　Consolidation
五、巩固练习

A Match the terms in column A with the definitions in column B.

A	B
1. Rebate	A. Any expenses during the stay except the room expense.
2. Direct Bill	B. A payment card issued to users as a system of payment. It allows the cardholder to pay for goods and services based on the holder's promise to pay for them.
3. Incidentals	C. Free Independent Traveler
4. Credit Card	D. A reduction made on guest's bill, usually with management's approval.
5. FIT	E. Guest's expenses are sent to a designated payer (usually his or her company) for settlement.

B Translation

i. Translate the following sentences into Chinese.

1. This is the bill for your room charges (房费) and this one is for incidentals (杂费).
2. Did you sign any bills in the last hour, or take anything from the mini-bar (小冰箱) this morning?
3. Madam, we took 800 RMB authorization (预授权) before. Your consumption is 650 RMB. We'll complete the charge within it.
4. I understand you booked a car to the airport at 7:00. The shuttle bus to the airport will be parking at the entrance to the lobby (大厅) at 6:50.
5. The Revenue Manager's job is to maximize the revenue (收益最大化) per available room by selling rooms to the right customers, at the right price, at the right time.

ii. Translate the following sentences into English.
1. 格林先生，今天早晨您是否用过酒店服务设施（hotel service），或在餐厅用过早餐？
2. 这几天您的朋友与您同住（share the room with）费用怎么办呢？您要平均分担费用（split the bill）吗？
3. 我们酒店退房时间（check-out）是中午12点钟，如果您希望晚上六点付账，需要付一晚的费用。
4. 行李领班（bell captain）会把行李放在储藏室。当您准备离开的时候，您可以向他索要（claim luggage）行李。
5. 机场巴士就停在酒店入口处（entrance）。祝旅途安全，欢迎（look forward to）下次光临。

 Writing

Questionnaire 征询意见表

A questionnaire is a simple, productive tool to aid you in obtaining constructive feedback from both existing and potential customers. As a manager or supervisor, you may ask guests to fill in the questionnaires on various occasions before they check out. Later, you should discuss the feedback with your colleagues to see what else the hotel can improve.

Suppose you are the Reception Manager, write a questionnaire using the following example. Ask your employees to place the copies on the table of the guest rooms or at Front Desk.

Outline:
1. Server's name
2. Date and time
3. Number of the guests
4. Categories of service:
   (1) Hospitality, (2) Food and service, (3) Environment

Example

Questionnaire

Thank you for taking time to complete this card

Date _____ time _____ ☐A.M ☐P.M
How many in your party? _____
Server's name _____

HOSPITALITY

Were you greeted as you entered? ☐YES ☐NO
Did the hostess/host seat you? ☐YES ☐NO

| Did server introduce her/himself by name? | ☐YES ☐NO |

FOOD AND SERVICE

Was food served promptly?	☐YES ☐NO
Was your order correct?	☐YES ☐NO
Was food properly prepared?	☐YES ☐NO
Did you receive smiling service?	☐YES ☐NO

ENVIRONMENT

Did our staff have a neat, clean appearance?	☐YES ☐NO
Were your dining area and dining utensils clean?	☐YES ☐NO
Was the restaurant clean overall?	☐YES ☐NO

Chapter 6
Housekeeping
客房部

Major Topics　一、酒店知识：Housekeeping Department 客房部
　　　　　　　　二、酒店员工：Room Attendant 客房清洁工
　　　　　　　　　　　　　　Houseperson 勤杂工
　　　　　　　　　　　　　　Public Area Attendant 公共区域清洁工
　　　　　　　　　　　　　　Linen and Uniform Room Attendant 布草制服房员工
　　　　　　　　三、酒店视频：Housekeeping Training for Professional Cleaners 客房部清洁工的专业培训
　　　　　　　　四、酒店对话：Scenario 1: P.M. Room Attendant's Routine 晚班客房服务员的日常工作
　　　　　　　　　　　　　　Scenario 2: Public Area Cleaning 公共区域保洁
　　　　　　　　　　　　　　Scenario 3: Housekeeping 客房服务
　　　　　　　　　　　　　　Scenario 4: Turn-down Service 夜床服务
　　　　　　　　五、巩固练习

　　The main topic of this chapter is the operations of Housekeeping Department. In *Part One*, you'll read ABC about the housekeeping. In *Part Two*, job description of working staff is provided for you to have some basics about the responsibility of each job in the department. In *Part Three*, you'll watch a short video about the housekeeping training for professional cleaners. In the next section, *Part Four* will provide situational dialogues for you to practice the skills related to housekeeping through making situational dialogues. *Part Five* includes some additional exercises to enhance your knowledge and skills of the department.

Part One ABC for Hotel
一、酒店知识

Housekeeping Department 客房部

Word Tips

aesthetic /iːsˈθetɪk/ adj. 美的；美学的
linen /ˈlɪnɪn/ n. 亚麻布，亚麻织品
streamline /ˈstriːmlaɪn/ v. 使合理化
clump /klʌmp/ n. 块，丛
fragile /ˈfrædʒaɪl/ adj. 脆的；易碎的
ammonia /əˈməʊnɪə/ n. [化]氨
bleach /bliːtʃ/ n. 漂白剂
scum /skʌm/ n. 浮渣；泡沫
blight /blaɪt/ n. 枯萎病；荒芜
dumpster /ˈdʌmpstə(r)/ n. 大垃圾桶
shampooer /ʃæmˈpuː(r)/ n. 地毯清洗机
alter /ˈɔːltə(r)/ v. 使变形

appeal /əˈpiːl/ n. 吸引力，感染力
contractor /kənˈtræktə(r)/ n. 承包商
vacuum /ˈvækjʊəm/ v. 吸尘
crumb /krʌm/ n. 碎屑
mantle /ˈmæntle/ n. 地幔；覆盖物
disinfectant /ˌdɪsɪnˈfektənt/ n. 消毒剂
sink /sɪŋk/ n. 水槽
lime /laɪm/ n. 石灰；酸橙
tub /tʌb/ n. 浴盆；桶
blinds /blaɪndz/ n. 百叶窗
solvent /ˈsɒlvənt/ n. 溶剂
erode /ɪˈrəʊd/ v. 腐蚀

Efficiently managed Housekeeping Departments ensure the cleanliness, maintenance, and aesthetic appeal of hotels. The Housekeeping Department not only prepares clean guestrooms on a timely basis for arriving guests, it also cleans and maintains everything in the hotel so that the property is as fresh and attractive as the day it opened for business.

Housekeeping Department usually has more employees than any other hotel departments. Besides the management staff, there are employees assigned to clean guestrooms, public spaces, back-of-the-house areas, meeting rooms, and banquet rooms. Some hotels have employees working in night cleaning and linen and laundry rooms, while in the other hotels, these areas are covered by contractors.

The tasks performed by a Housekeeping Department are critical to the smooth daily operation of any hotel. The primary communications of Housekeeping Department are with Front Office Department and Maintenance Department. At most properties, the reception agent is not allowed to assign guestrooms until the rooms have been cleaned, inspected and released by the Housekeeping Department. Maintenance Department has similar goals and methods as Housekeeping Department. Hence, a close working relationship is very important.

How to perform routine housekeeping duties? Here are some suggestions:

Step 1: Start your housekeeping duties in the bathrooms. Bathrooms often require allowing cleaning products such as shower and toilet bowl cleaners to "soak in" for a period of 10 to 15 minutes. Applying cleaning products in the bathrooms first will streamline your housekeeping duties by allowing you to move on and complete other areas of the home or room while the cleaning products to do their job.

Step 2: Clean or dust furniture and other hard surfaces such as counter tops. Complete this step before cleaning or vacuuming floors. Imagine vacuuming a rug and then having a large clump of dust, crumbs or dirt fall onto the freshly cleaned area. Check with your employer to find out if any furniture item or surface is fragile or has special cleaning needs. Generally, you should use a standard wood furniture polish for coffee tables, picture frames and fireplace mantles. Use either a standard or non-ammonia, eco-friendly glass cleaner to clean mirrors and glass table tops. A disinfectant cleanser containing bleach or an antibacterial agent should be used on kitchen and bathroom counter tops and sinks. Use a feather duster or Swiffer duster to remove dust from ceiling fans and blinds.

Step 3: Return to the bathroom and clean the shower, toilet, counters and mirrors. Pay special attention to hard water spots, soap scum or lime buildup in the shower. Your employer will expect that you will remove these blights from shower walls and tubs. Use a sponge or a Magic Eraser in addition to traditional shower cleaning products. When cleaning the toilet, be sure to wipe around the bottom base of the fixture in addition to cleaning out the inside with toilet bowl cleaner and a brush.

Step 4: Empty all trash cans throughout the home or room. Check the kitchen, bathrooms, bedrooms and home office. Replace trash bags in all garbage cans and discard waste appropriately in a dumpster, outside trash container or recycling bin.

Step 5: Clean all floors by vacuuming or sweeping and mopping. This step should be the last duty that you perform before you leave. It doesn't make sense to clean floors first and then track additional dirt and mud across them while you perform the rest of your cleaning duties. Your employer may have specific equipment such as vacuum cleaners, carpet shampooers or special floor cleaning products on site for you to use. If this is not the case, you will need to provide your own supplies. Before you begin any floor-cleaning task which involves cleaning solvents or chemicals, discuss which products should be used with your employer. Certain flooring surfaces such as Pergo, hardwood, and certain natural tiles will be altered or eroded by the use of chemical cleaners.

Based on the above passage, decide whether the following statements are true or false. Write T for true and F for false.

1. _____ Housekeeping Department is only responsible for cleaning guestrooms.
2. _____ Housekeeping Department usually has more employees than any other hotel department.
3. _____ Housekeeping works closer to Front Office than to Maintenance Department.
4. _____ Room attendant should use a wood furniture polish for tables, picture frames or fireplace mantles.
5. _____ After cleaning the sitting room the room attendant should clean the shower, toilet,

counters and mirrors in the bathroom.

6. _____ It doesn't make sense to use a feather duster to remove dust from ceiling fans first and then vacuum floors.

Part Two   Working Staff
二、酒店员工

1 Listen to the job description of each one in the department, correct the mistakes and put the right ones in the blanks.

(1) **Room Attendant** performs routine duties of cleaning rest rooms and bath rooms under supervision of the supervisor.
   a. _____
   b. _____
   中文提示：
      客房清洁工：每日清洁客房和浴室，并接受主管检查。

(2) **Houseperson** fulfills the tasks such as collecting dirty linen for washing, receives linen supplies, stores linen supplies in floor linen closets, replenishes towel trolley, remove trash collected by room attendants etc. in order to maintain guest rooms, working areas and the hotel premises in general in a clean and orderly manner.
   a. _____
   b. _____
中文提示：
      勤杂工：负责收集脏布草送洗，接收干净布草，在每层楼的布草间储存布草，补充清洁车装备，收客房里清理出的垃圾等，保证客房、工作区域干净整洁。

(3) **Public Area Attendant** keeps all public areas and public equipment (such as lobby restrooms, telephone areas, the Reception and the offices of departments in the hotel) in a neat and orderly condition.
   a. _____
   b. _____
   中文提示：
      公共区域清洁工：负责保持公共区域以及公共设备（例如大堂洗手间、公用电话区、前台、各部门办公室等）干净整洁。

(4) **Linen and Uniform Attendant** stores and issues uniforms, bed sheets and table linen, and also takes orders and maintains linen room supplies.
   a. _____

b. _____

中文提示：

布草制服房员工：储存、发放制服、床单、桌布等，统计库存并保证布草房供给。

2 Listen again and discuss the job description of the post you wish to hold in your career.

Part Three   Video for the Hotel
三、酒店视频

Housekeeping Training for Professional Cleaners 客房部清洁工的专业培训

Useful Words and Expressions

premise /ˈpremɪs/ n. 前提；经营场址
disposal /dɪˈspəʊzl/ n. 处理
preserve /prɪˈzɜːv/ v. 保存；保护
allergy /ˈælədʒi/ n. 过敏症
neutral /ˈnjuːtrəl/ adj. 中立的，中性的
fabric /ˈfæbrɪk/ n. 织物；布
splash /splæʃ/ n. 飞溅的水；污点
sanitary /ˈsænətri/ adj. 卫生的，清洁的

hazard /ˈhæzəd/ n. 危险，冒险
litter /ˈlɪtə(r)/ n. 垃圾
pristine /ˈprɪstiːn/ adj. 原始的，纯朴的
infection /ɪnˈfekʃn/ n. 感染；传染
liquid /ˈlɪkwɪd/ n. 液体，流体
sanative /ˈsænətɪv/ adj. 有益健康的
ventilate /ˈventɪleɪt/ v. 使通风
smudge /smʌdʒ/ n. 污点，污迹

A Watch the video twice, and decide whether the following statements are true or false according to the video.

1. _____ The video tells us that the first impression is of great importance to housekeeping as well as to the guests in the hotel.
2. _____ Housekeeping can reduce the level of pests and insects and minimize the spread of bacteria and infection, but cannot help those who have allergies.
3. _____ Cleaning products that are color-coded blue indicate they should be used in different cleaning areas.
4. _____ The Room Attendant should start the dirty areas, then clean areas that are dirtier; this can minimize the dirt to cleaner areas.
5. _____ Always start at the bottom and walk down so any splashes of cleaning solution are cleaned away.

B Watch the video again, and answer the following questions.

1. How could the regular and effective cleaning help preserve the furniture in the hotel?
   _____.

2. For the safety purpose, what should the Room Attendant do before cleaning the room?
   _____.

3. What cleaning product does Jangro provide for housekeeping?
   _____.

4. How do you understand it's a good idea to plan what to do before starting on any cleaning task?
   _____.

5. Which one do you think the Room Attendant should clean first? The door handles, the floor or the light switchers?
   _____.

Part Four　Dialogues in the Hotel
四、酒店对话

Scenario 1

P.M. Room Attendant's Routine 晚班客房服务员的日常工作

A Listen to Dialogue 1, and complete the following conversation with what you hear.

Alex(A): So in P.M. shift, our main task is to perform turndown service.
Karen(K): That's right.
A: What kind of (1) _____ needs turndown service?
K: All stay-over rooms, rooms checked in already and rooms with (2)_____.
A: I see. What do we do during turndown?
K: We briefly clean the bathroom and restock it with fresh towels, rotate or (3) _____, tidy the guestroom, empty trash bins, fold back the bedspread, blanket and top sheet, (4)_____ and draw the drapes.
A: That's a long list!
K: The fact is that turndown service normally doesn't need a lot of time. Sometimes we can (5)_____ as many as 20 rooms per hour.
A: Cool!
K: One more thing, some hotels will put a small (6)_____ on the pillow to wish guest "sweet dreams."
A: That's lovely. What else do we do at (7)_____?
K: We may need to provide additional amenities like extra towels, or other types of special

Chapter 6　Housekeeping 客房部

61

amenities like hair dryer, (8) _____, spot removers etc. Or sometimes there are guestrooms requesting extra cleaning service.

B Divide your class into groups of two or three students, and do the dialogue again.

Scenario 2

Public Area Cleaning 公共区域保洁

A Listen to Dialogue 2 and write numbers in the blanks to show the correct order of the conversation.

_____. **Alex(A):** Where else then?

_____. **A:** Of course not.

_____. **Karen(K):** Let me see...front-of-the-house areas such as elevators, public restrooms, pool and patio areas, exercise room, spa area, meeting rooms, dining rooms, banquet rooms, convention exhibit halls etc., back-of-the-house areas such as management offices, storage areas, Linen and Uniform Room, Laundry, employee locker rooms etc.

_____. **A:** I see. What should we pay attention to while cleaning?

_____. **K:** Well, that depends. For example, lobby is a heavy traffic area and the gateway to the hotel, so it requires continual cleaning. Meeting rooms and banquet rooms we only clean before and after using. We only pick up trash from management office twice a day and vacuum them every three days. Of course, the frequency of cleaning different areas may vary in different hotels.

_____. **A:** Good morning, Karen. We'll clean the public area, and that means we'll work in the hotel lobby all day. Is that right?

_____. **K:** I guess the most important thing is try to avoid disturbing guests. For instance, you cannot drive everyone out of restroom because you need to clean it.

_____. **A:** That's really a lot.

_____. **K:** Not exactly. Although lobby is a very important part of public area, it isn't the only part.

_____. **K:** You're right. We are literally taking care of the whole hotel except guestrooms.

_____. **A:** How often do we clean these areas?

B Role play: One student plays the role of Alex while another plays the role of Karen.

Scenario 3

Housekeeping 客房服务

A Listen to Dialogue 3 and fill in the table with correct information.

Gender of the guest	Service Dept.	Service time	Service offered

B Listen to the dialogue again, and do a situational dialogue with your partner.

Room Attendant(R): Housekeeping. May I come in?
Guest(G): Yes, please.
R: When would you like me to do your room, sir?
G: You can do it now if you like. I was just about to go down for my breakfast when you came. But before you start, would you do this for me?
R: Yes, what is it?
G: I would like you to go and get me a flask of hot water. I need some hot water to wash down medicine after breakfast.
R: I'm sorry that your flask is empty. I'll go and get you another flask that's full at once.
G: Thank you.
R: I'll be right back.

Scenario 4

Turn-down Service 夜床服务

A Listen to Dialogue 4 and mark the following sentences with T (true) or F (false).
1. _____ It was time for the room attendant to do the room service, but the guest refused.
2. _____ The guest requested the room attendant to come back in three hours because he would treat his friends.
3. _____ The guest wanted to have the bathroom cleaned because he just had a shower and the bathroom was in a mess.
4. _____ The room attendant drew the curtains to have a very pleasant setting for the guests.

B Listen to the dialogue again and answer the following questions.
1. Why did the guest deny the turn-down service?

2. Why did the guest ask the room attendant to tidy up a bit in the bathroom?

3. What would the guest do with a bottle of boiled water?

4. What other services did the room attendant offer to the guests?

Room Attendant(R): Good evening, sir. May I do the turn-down service for you now?
Guest(G): Oh, thank you. But you see, we are having some friends over. We're going to have a small party here in the room. Could you come back in three hours?
R: Certainly, sir. I'll let the overnight staff know. They will come then.
G: That's fine. Well, our friends seem to be a little late. Would you tidy up a bit in the bathroom? I've just taken a bath and it is quite a mess now. Besides, please bring us a bottle of just boiled water. We'd treat our guests to typical Chinese tea.
R: Yes, sir. I'll bring in some fresh towels together with the drinking water.
G: Okay.
R: (*Having done all on request.*) It's growing dark. Would you like me to draw the curtains for you, sir?
G: Why not? That would be so cozy.
R: May I turn on the lights for you?
G: Yes, please. I'd like to do some reading while waiting.
R: Yes, sir. Is there anything I can do for you?
G: No more. You're a smart girl indeed. Thank you very much.
R: I'm always at your service. Goodbye, sir, and do have a very pleasant evening.

Additional Exercises:

Divide the class into groups. Each group makes a situational dialogue using words or phrases for housekeeping. You may refer to the working procedures or sentence patterns in Dialogue 1, Dialogue 2, Dialogue 3 and Dialogue 4.

Additional Words and Phrases 更多的词汇短语储备

Word Tips

clothes-hanger 衣架	hard mattress 硬床垫	shampoo 洗发水
pillow 枕头	soft mattress 软床垫	conditioner 护发素
pillow case 枕袋	laundry list 洗衣单	toothbrush 牙刷
quilt 被子	laundry bag 洗衣袋	toothpaste 牙膏

tissues 面巾纸 bath robe 浴袍 writing paper 信纸
toilet paper 卫生纸 hairdryer 吹风机 wardrobe 衣柜
bath tub 浴缸 coffee table 茶几 vanity/dressing table 梳妆台
face towel 小方巾 bed-head 床头 bed cover 床罩
bath mat 地巾 electric kettle 电热水壶
shower cap 浴帽 slippers 拖鞋

Part Five   Consolidation
五、巩固练习

A Match the terms in column A with the definitions in column B.

A	B
1. occupied	A. The room has been cleaned and inspected and is ready for an arriving guest.
2. check-out	B. A report prepared each night by a reception agent who lists rooms occupied that night and indicates guests who are expected to check out the following day.
3. recycle inventories	C. Items are consumed or used up during the course of routine housekeeping operations.
4. Do not disturb.	D. The room has been cleaned, but not yet inspected for an arriving guest.
5. due out	E. Turn down guest bed sheets and refresh the guestroom for the evening.
6. vacant and clean	F. The guest has requested not to be disturbed.
7. out-of-order	G. The room is expected to become vacant after the following day's check-out time.
8. stayover	H. The room cannot be assigned to a guest. A room may be out-of-order for a variety of reasons, including the need for maintenance, refurbishing, and extensive cleaning.
9. turndown	I. Items that have relatively limited useful lives but that are used over and over again in housekeeping operations.
10. occupancy report	J. The guest has settled his or her account, returned the room keys, and left the hotel.
11. non-recycled inventories	K. The guest is not checking out today and will remain at least one more night.
12. vacant and ready	L. A guest has currently registered to the room.

B **Role play: Laundry Service**

When the guest needs the laundry service you should check the guest room number, name, payment term and washing method. You must check if the clothes have been damaged or stained, check if the bottoms fall off, and check if any items have been left over in the pocket. Besides, you must read the laundry labels carefully before you do your laundry.

Situation 1: Suppose you are the room attendant who collects the laundry bag for Mr. Green in Room 2505. Make a situational dialogue based on phrases or sentence patterns you've learnt.

Situation 2: Suppose you are the Housekeeping Supervisor, give a lecture to train the housekeeping staff how to identify the laundry labels on the clothes and how to wash the clothes accordingly.

	Dry clean	干洗
	Do not dry clean	不可干洗
	Iron	熨烫
	Iron on low/ medium/ high heat	低温熨烫（100℃）/ 中温熨烫（150℃）/ 高温熨烫（100℃）
	Do not iron	不可熨烫
	Bleach/do not bleach	可漂白/不可漂白
	Dry/hang dry/dry flat	悬挂晾干/随洗随干/平放晾干
	Line dry	洗涤
	Wash with cold/warm/ hot water	冷水/温水/热水机洗
	Hand wash only	只能手洗
	Do not wash	不可洗涤
	Tumble dry with low heat	低温转笼干燥
	Tumble dry with medium heat	中温转笼干燥
	Tumble dry with high heat	高温转笼干燥
	Do not tumble dry	不可转笼干燥

C **Translation**

i. Translate the following sentences into Chinese.
1. Housekeeping Department (客房部) usually has more employees than any other hotel departments.
2. The tasks performed by the Housekeeping Department are critical to (对……重要) the smooth daily operation of any hotel.
3. Today we need to change bed sheets for 17 king rooms (大床) and 23 twin rooms. We have to work overtime (加班).

4. When would you like me to do your room (打扫房间), sir? I can do it right now if you like.
5. We could offer many different services, such as washing, dry-cleaning, ironing (熨烫) and mending.

ii. Translate the following sentences into English.
1. 在客人离开之前尽量不要去打扰(disturb)。如果必须,需敲门三下,看看屋里有什么反应(respond)。
2. 还有个问题,一旦发现房间有损坏(damages),我们该怎么办?
3. 有些酒店会在客人枕头上(on the pillow)放一小块巧克力,以此祝愿客人有"甜美的梦"。
4. 事实上,夜床服务(turn-down service)通常不会花很长时间。我们会应客人要求(on request)提前做好。
5. 我房间的卫生间有些问题(be something wrong with)。味道很不好。你能来看看吗?

 Writing

Laundry Registration 洗衣登记表

Many quality hotels offer laundry services for their guests. Both laundry and dry cleaning services are available. Same-day turnaround is standard service provided by hotel laundry, if it is received before the time indicated. The cost of the service will vary between hotel chains, but the process for using the service is fairly standard.

Suppose you're the guest in the hotel, and you want to have your clothes washed or ironed, fill out the laundry registration, tick out items, and leave it on the table of your room. The room attendant will take it away when she comes to do the housekeeping.

Laundry Registration

Kunming Shangri-la Hotel   *No.*

Name:		PLEASE TICK ONE
Signature:		☐ REGULAR SERVICE—GARMENTS RECEIVED BEFORE 10:00 A.M. RETURNED THE SAMEDAY
Date	Room No.	☐ EXPRESS SERVICE—GARMENTS RECEVED BEFORE 2:00 P.M. RETURNED THE SAMEDAY

SPECIAL SERVICE: ☐ REPAIRING   ☐ BUTTONING   ☐ STAIN-REMOVING

GUEST COUNT	HOTEL COUNT	LADIES	UNIT PRICE(¥)	AMOUNT
		BLOUSE	4.00	
		BRASSIERE	2.00	
		DRESS	8.00	
		HANDKERCHIEF	1.00	
		EVENING DRESS	10.00	
		UNDERPANTS	2.00	
		PAJAMAS	4.00	
		SHORTS	4.00	
		SKIRT	15.00	
		SLACKS	6.00	
		SOCKS	1.00	
		STOCKINGS	1.00	
		SUIT	15.00	
		SWEATER	9.00	
		T-SHIRT	3.00	
		UNDERSHIRT	2.00	

GUEST	HOTEL COUNT	GENTLEMEN	UNIT PRICE(¥)	AMOUNT
		BATHROBE	5.00	
		DRESS SHIRT	1.00	
		NORMAL SHIRT	4.00	
		SWIMSHORT	6.00	
		TROUSERS	3.00	
		VEST	4.00	
		SPORTS SHIRT	10.00	
		WAFUKU	9.00	

1. GUEST IS REQUIRED TO COMPLETE LIST OTHERWISE HOTEL COUNT MUST BE ACCEPTED AS CORRECT.
2. THE HOTEL IS NOT RESPONSIBLE FOR VALUABLES IN POCKETS.
3. IN CASE OF LOSS OR DAMAGE THE HOTEL WILL BE LIABLE TO NO MORE THAN TEN TIMES THE REGULAR PROCESSING CHARGE OF THE ITEM.
4. ALL CLAIMS MUST BE MADE WITHIN 24 HOURS AFTER DELIVERY AND MUST BE ACCOMPANIED BY THE ORIGINAL LIST.

SPECIAL INSTRUCTIONS
BASIC CHARGE ¥_____
50% EXTRA CHARGE FOR EXPRESS ¥_____
10% SERVICE CHARGE ¥_____
GRAND TOTAL ¥_____
BILLED BY:

Chapter 7
Food and Beverage
餐饮服务

Major Topics
一、酒店知识：What We Eat 吃的学问
二、酒店员工：Food and Beverage Manager 餐饮部经理
　　　　　　　Restaurant Manager 餐厅经理
　　　　　　　Restaurant Hostess 餐厅女招待
三、酒店视频：Types of Glassware 酒杯的种类
四、酒店对话：Scenario 1: Reservation for a Table 订座
　　　　　　　Scenario 2: Taking Orders 订餐
　　　　　　　Scenario 3: Buffet 自助餐
　　　　　　　Scenario 4: In the Bar 泡酒吧
五、巩固练习

This chapter centers on the topic of food and beverage in the hotel restaurant. In *Part One*, you'll learn what people eat in the world as a warming-up exercise. In *Part Two*, job description of working staff is provided for you to have some basics about the responsibility of each job in the department. In *Part Three*, you'll watch a short video about types of glassware and learn how to use them when you serve the guests. In the next section, *Part Four* will provide some situational dialogues for you to practice the relevant skills and service based on different scenarios. *Part Five* includes additional exercises to enhance your knowledge and skills of dining or working in a restaurant.

Part One ABC for Hotel
一、酒店知识

What We Eat 吃的学问

Word Tips

Eskimo /ˈeskɪməʊ/ n. 爱斯基摩人
vegetarian /ˌvedʒəˈteərɪən/ n. 素食者
mash /mæʃ/ v. 捣碎
pie /paɪ/ n. 馅饼
onion /ˈʌnjən/ n. 洋葱
sauce /sɔːs/ n. 酱汁

North Pole /nɔːθ pəʊl/ n. 北极
soup /suːp/ n. 汤
Boston /ˈbɒstən/ n. 波士顿
hamburger /ˈhæmbɜːgə(r)/ n. 汉堡
lettuce /ˈletɪs/ n. 生菜
mustard /ˈmʌstəd/ n. 芥末

People in different parts of the world have very different ideas about what is good to eat. If you were an Eskimo near the North Pole, you would enjoy the raw meat from seals. If you were a nomad in the desert, you would prefer the roasted meat of sheep and goats. Americans cook the meat of many different animals, but perhaps their favorite meat is steak. Some people in India do not eat meat or fish at all. They are called vegetarians.

Even when people in different parts of the world eat the same food, they often prepare it very differently. If you were in Germany, you would find soup that is thick and heavy. If you were in China, you would find soup that is thin and clear. If you asked some Americans how they like their steak cooked, you would get a variety of answers. Some like their steak well-done, whereas others like it rare. Many prefer their steak medium—that is, halfway between rare and well-done. The Irish like plain boiled potatoes, whereas most Americans prefer their potatoes prepared in other ways—fried, baked, or boiled and then mashed and served with gravy.

People living in different regions of the same country often prepare foods differently. The United States has its regional specialties, too—for example, "southern fried chicken" and the baked beans of Boston. But there are national foods, too. For example, there are two desserts you would probably find anywhere in the United States. One is ice cream, and the other is apple pie. And all American children like hot dogs and hamburgers "plain"—with nothing on them. Others like theirs "with everything"—with onions, lettuce, fresh tomatoes, and sauces such as ketchup and mustard. The hamburger is the favorite quick lunch of most Americans.

Based on the above passage, decide whether the following statements are true or false. Write T for true and F for false.

1. _____ An Eskimo near the North Pole would enjoy the well-done meat from seals.

2. _____ People who do not eat meat are called vegetarians.
3. _____ Both the Irish and most Americans like boiled potatoes.
4. _____ Southern fried chicken is one of the national foods in America.
5. _____ The hamburger and hot dogs are the favorite quick lunch of most Americans.

Part Two   Working Staff
二、酒店员工

1 Listen to the job description of each one in the department, correct the mistakes and put the right ones in the blanks.

(1) **Food and Beverage Manager** oversees the operations of the kitchen, bar, dining room and other food outlets in a hotel. His major responsibilities include:

To ensure the required profitable market.
To update wine lists and menus.
To restock food materials.
To be responsible for marketing and sale advertisement.
To ensure that business is conducted in accordance with local and national food safety standards.
To hire and train staff.

　　a. _____
　　b. _____

中文提示：

　　餐饮部经理：监管酒店厨房、酒吧、餐厅和其他餐饮点的经营管理，其主要职责是确保利润目标，更新酒水单和菜单，采购食品原料，负责市场营销和广告促销，确保按地方和国家食品安全标准营业，雇用和培训员工。

(2) **Restaurant Manager** reports to Food and Beverage Manager, taking charge of daily operations of the restaurant. His major responsibilities are:

To regulate business operations.
To resolve customer issues.
To assign the staff jobs.
To monitor and evaluate employee performances.
To train staff.
To monitor inventory (ordering/ delivery).
To meet health and safe standard.

　　a. _____
　　b. _____

中文提示：

餐厅经理：向餐饮部经理汇报，主管餐厅的日常工作，其主要职责是管理餐厅经营活动，处理顾客投诉，分配工作任务，监管和考评员工，培训员工，负责库存和财产管理(采购和交付)，确保卫生安全达标。

(3) Restaurant Hostess

To take reservations, manage seating arrangement and contact guests.

To receive guests, including checking reservation information, assigning tables and waling the guests.

To take orders, answer questions about the menu and do other helpful things.

a. _____

b. _____

中文提示：

餐厅女招待：负责餐厅的预订、桌位的安排和客户的联络工作等；负责客人的接待工作，包括核对预订记录、安排座位、引客人入座；请客人点菜，解释菜单，做其他行政工作。

2 Listen again and discuss the job description of the post you wish to hold in your career.

Part Three　Video for the Hotel
三、酒店视频

Types of Glassware 酒杯的种类

Useful Words and Expressions	
flute /fluːt/ n. 香槟笛	pony /ˈpəʊnɪ/ n. 甜酒杯
snifter /ˈsnɪftə(r)/ n. 矮脚小口大肚酒杯	highball glass /ˈhaɪbɔːl glass/ n. 什饮杯
sparking /spɑːkɪŋ/ adj. 起泡的	aroma /əˈrəʊmə/ n. 芳香
ounce /aʊns/ n. 盎司	extra /ˈekstrə/ adj. 附加的
vessel /ˈvesl/ n. 容器	champagne /ʃæmˈpeɪn/ n. 香槟
brandy /ˈbrændɪ/ n. 白兰地	aperitif /əˌperəˈtiːf/ n. 开胃酒
pour /pɔː(r)/ v. 倒	Scotch /skɒtʃ/ n. 苏格兰威士忌
plethora /ˈpleθərə/ n. 过多	cocktail /ˈkɒkteɪl/ n. 鸡尾酒

A Watch the video twice, and decide whether the following statements are true or false according to the video.

1. _____ The topic of the video is the categories of the glassware, including a wine glass, a flute, a pony, a snifter, and a highball glass.
2. _____ The wine glass can be used to contain red wines, white wines, or even whisky.
3. _____ The flute is a kind of instrument which is designed for champagnes as well as sparkling wines.
4. _____ The snifter is used for brandies as well as many different types of aperitifs, and dessert wines.
5. _____ There are different types of beverage glasses available, but only four of them are used by the bar to run the business.

B Watch the video again, and answer the following questions.

1. What is the main glassware used by the bar to run the business?
   _____.
2. What wines can bring the aroma up out the nose very easily?
   _____.
3. To get a good amount of wine without completely destroying all the extra air in the vessel, how much capacity will be appropriate?
   _____.
4. The pony is used for port wines. What else can it be used for?
   _____.
5. Which kind of glassware is used for neat pours, scotches, whiskeys and plethora of cocktails?
   _____.

Part Four　Dialogues in the Hotel
四、酒店对话

Scenario 1

Reservation for a Table 订座

A Listen to Dialogue 1 and decide whether the following statements are true or false according to the dialogue.

1. _____ The guest has no reservation beforehand.
2. _____ The waiter chooses a table by the door for the guest.
3. _____ It's quite well for the guest to have a good view of the city.

4. _____ As the table is near the band platform, the guest deems that it'll be noisy.
5. _____ The guest is reluctant to accept the waiter's advice, so he changes to another table.

B Listen to the dialogue again and answer the following questions.

1. How many people does the guest reserve for?
   _____

2. Which table does the waiter choose for the guest?
   _____

3. What does the guest worry about?
   _____

4. Does the guest change to another table? Why?
   _____

Waitress (W): Good evening, sir. Do you have a reservation?
Guest (G): Yes, I have the reservation for four people, and my name is Johnny Depp.
W: Yes, sir. This way, please. We've chosen a table for you by the window. Is that all right, sir?
G: Certainly. It's quite good.
W: You are welcome, sir. This position has a good view of the city.
G: Uh...but this table is near the band platform. Is it going to be very noisy when the band plays some music?
W: Oh, don't worry, sir. The sound of the music is quite soft. We'll not bring you any inconvenience.
G: Are you sure? I'll have a talk with my friends. I hate being annoyed by the pop music.
W: Could you stay and listen to it for a while? If you don't like it, we'll find another table for you.
G: That's great. You give a good service indeed.

Scenario 2

Taking Orders 订餐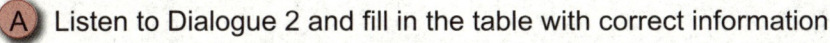

A Listen to Dialogue 2 and fill in the table with correct information.

Today's special	Order for appetizer	Order for main course	Order for dessert	Order for drink

B Listen to the dialogue again. One student raises the questions according to the service sequence for order of the food while others answer the questions.

1. _____
2. _____
3. _____
4. _____

Waitress (W): Hi, my name is Mary and I'll be your waitress for this evening. How are you this evening?

Jason (J): We're very well, thank you.

W: Let me tell you about today's specials. We have fried chicken with boiled potatoes and the soup of the day is vegetable soup. Are you ready to order or do you want me to come back?

J: We're ready now. We have read the menu.

W: OK, what would you like for your appetizer?

J: We would both like soup of the day.

W: OK, and what would you like for your main course?

J: I'll have a pizza and my wife will have a lamb.

W: OK. Would you like to order dessert now or would you like to wait?

J: I think we'll wait. If we are hungry, then we'll order dessert.

W: OK. Can I get you something to drink?

J: Can we have a bottle of red wine?

W: Yes, that's no problem. I'll go and get your drinks now.

Scenario 3

Buffet 自助餐

A Listen to Dialogue 3 and complete the following conversation.

Waiter (W): Welcome to Buffet City. How can I help you?

Jane (J): I'd like to know what your (1) _____ is like.

W: It's got an (2) _____ salad bar.

J: Do you have hot and (3) _____?

W: Yes, and we have a wide variety of (4) _____ to choose from.

J: Do you have any soup?

W: Yes, we have three different kinds of soup today.

J: What kind of soup do you have?

W: Today, we have (5) _____, spicy bean and onion soup.

J: What kind of main meals do you have on your buffet?

W: We have pizza, pasta and lasagna.

J: What about sides?
W: We have French fries, (6) _____, and chicken wings.
J: That sounds good. We'll take two.

B Listen to the dialogue again, and do a situational dialogue with your partner.

Scenario 4

In the Bar 泡酒吧

A Listen to Dialogue 4, and write down the relevant information you hear.

1. Liquors available: _____
2. Soft drinks available: _____
3: Order of John: _____
4. Order of April: _____
5. Brand of the beer: _____

B Divide your class into groups of two or three students, and do the dialogue again.

Bartender (B): Good evening. Would you like something to drink?
John (J): Yes, but give us a couple of minutes to look at the drink list first.
B: Sure, sir. Please take your time.
J: Let's see. Champagne, beer, whisky, cocktail... I'd like some iced beer. What about you, April?
April (A): You're kidding, John. You know I don't drink liquor.
B: We have a variety of soda water and fruit juice. Would you like something soft to drink, madam?
A: Certainly. What kind of fruit juice do you have?
B: Plum juice, orange juice, carrot juice, pineapple juice, lime juice and tomato juice.
A: I'll have lime juice.
B: Any special brand of the beer, sir?
J: Budweiser. One can will do.
B: Good. A can of Budweiser and a glass of lime juice. Just a moment, please.

Additional Exercises:

Divide the class into groups. Each group makes a situational dialogue using words or phrases for the Food and Beverage. You may refer to the working procedures or sentence patterns in Dialogue 1, Dialogue 2, Dialogue 3 and Dialogue 4.

Additional Words and Phrases 更多的词汇短语储备

1. 中餐

猪肉类 Pork
干锅排骨鸡：Griddle Cooked Spare Ribs and Chicken
咕噜肉：Gulaorou (Sweet and Sour Pork with Pineapple)
木耳肉片：Sautéed Sliced Pork with Black Fungus

牛肉类 Beef
干煸牛肉丝：Sautéed Shredded Beef in Chili Sauce
米粉牛肉：Steamed Beef with Rice Flour
铁板牛肉：Sizzling Beef Steak

海鲜类 Seafood
XO酱莲藕炒海螺片：Sautéed Sliced Sea Whelks and Lotus Root in XO Sauce
锅仔泡椒煮鲈鱼：Perch Stewed with Marinated Chili
葱姜肉蟹：Sautéed Crab with Ginger and Scallion

2. 西餐

牛肉类 Beef
牛里脊扒配黑椒少司 Grilled Beef Tenderloin with Black Pepper Sauce
扒肉眼牛排 Grilled Beef Rib-Eye Steak
西冷牛排配红酒少司 Roast Beef Sirloin Steak with Red Wine Sauce

海鲜类 Seafood
巴黎黄油烤龙虾 Baked Lobster with Garlic Butter
奶酪汁龙虾 Gratinated Lobster in Mornay Sauce
香炸西班牙鱿鱼圈 Deep-Fried Squid Rings

汤类 Soup
意大利蔬菜汤 Minestrone Soup
蔬菜干豆汤 Hearty Lentil Soup
牛油梨冻汤 Chilled Avocado Soup

Part Five Consolidation
五、巩固练习

A Choose the right glassware for the wine and complete the matching exercise.

Kinds of glassware	Types of wine
1. a wine glass	A. dessert wines
2. a flute	B. brandies
3. a pony	C. whiskeys
4. a snifter	D. champagnes
5. a highball glass	E. sparkling wines
	F. red wine

B Translation

i. Translate the following sentences into Chinese.

1. There is a music teahouse (音乐茶座) where you can enjoy both classical music such as Beethoven, Mozart, Liszt, and modern music, while having some Chinese tea or other soft drinks.
2. What would you like to drink? We've a great variety of wines. Which kind of them do you prefer (喜欢)?
3. I can offer you some oyster soup (牡蛎汤). Compliments of the chef.
4. Our appetizer (开胃菜) was served twenty minutes ago, but our main courses are not here yet.
5. We provide a set-menu dinner (套餐), buffet, barbeque or cocktail party. What do you prefer?

ii. Translate the following sentences into English.

1. 对不起，没有座位了。如果您不介意的话，我可以安排您与那边的女士同坐一桌(share a table)。
2. 您喜欢几成熟的牛排，熟透的(well done)，还是适中的(medium)，还是半生的(rare)呢？
3. 我们想吃点当地特色菜(local specials)，你能给我们提点建议吗？
4. 我尝着味道不对，太淡(weak)了，请帮我拿些盐。
5. 很抱歉，先生，我们只有两种啤酒，一种是烈度适中(medium-strength)的啤酒，另一种是出口啤酒。

Writing

Performance Review 绩效考核

Commenting on someone else's performance can be a difficult task, especially if the individual is not able to take it positively. The performance evaluation is aimed at assessing the employees to the best of their performance, and highlighting the areas of improvement if any. This is necessary not only for the hotel growth, but also for the overall growth of employees.

Suppose that you are the manager of Food & Beverage Department, conduct an annual performance review of your employee Wang Xiaolu based on the following indicators. Self review is part of a review, but assessment of other parties is more objective as well as reliable. As a manager of the department, you need to see to it that you are able to judge her performance effectively, considering both her negative and positive points.

Performance Review

Jinjiang Hotel, Chengdu

Name	Wang Xiaolu					Title		Consultant	
On Board Date	15/05/2020					Pass Date		16/05/2021	
Items	Self-Review					Supervisor/Manager Review			
	Excellent	Good	Average	Below	Poor	Excellent	Good	Average	Below	Poor
	5	4	3	2	1	5	4	3	2	1
Capability										
Attitude										
Professionalism										
Responsibility										
Team Work										
Time Management										
Communication										
Overview										
Self Assessment										
Supervisor/Manager Assessment										
Advice	Adjustment Of Salary					Adjustment Of Title				
GM Approval										

Chapter 8
Western Food
西式餐点

Major Topics
一、酒店知识：European Cuisine 欧洲菜
二、酒店员工：Restaurant Reception Manager 餐厅接待经理
　　　　　　　Headwaiter 餐厅领班
　　　　　　　Restaurant Cashier 餐厅收银员
三、酒店视频：Table Taboos for Western Cuisine 西餐餐桌上的禁忌
四、酒店对话：Scenario 1: Taking Orders 点菜
　　　　　　　Scenario 2: Serving Foods 上菜
　　　　　　　Scenario 3: American Breakfast 美式早餐
　　　　　　　Scenario 4: Change of the Food 换餐
五、巩固练习

> This chapter concentrates on the topic of serving Western foods in the hotel restaurant. In *Part One*, you'll read ABC about Western cuisine as a warming-up exercise. In *Part Two*, you'll understand the job description for the working staff who serve the Western foods in the hotel restaurant. In *Part Three*, you'll watch a short video about the table taboos for Western foods so that you can avoid mistakes when serving guests. In the next section, *Part Four* you'll do some situational dialogues to enhance your knowledge and skills of dining or working in a restaurant. *Part Five* includes additional exercises to enhance your knowledge and skills of serving Western foods.

Part One ABC for Hotel
一、酒店知识

European Cuisine 欧洲菜

Word Tips

cuisine /kwɪˈziːn/ n. 菜肴
continental /ˌkɒntɪˈnentl/ adj. 大陆的
substantial /səbˈstænʃl/ adj. 真正的
condiment /ˈkɒndɪmənt/ n. 佐料
pasta /ˈpæstə/ n. 意大利面食
starch /stɑːtʃ/ n. 淀粉质食物
dairy /ˈdeərɪ/ n. 奶制品

culinary /ˈkʌlɪnərɪ/ adj. 烹饪的
distinguish /dɪˈstɪŋgwɪʃ/ v. 区分；辨别
sauce /sɔːs/ n. 调味汁
seasoning /ˈsiːzənɪŋ/ n. 调味品
pastry /ˈpeɪstrɪ/ n. 点心；甜点
savory /ˈseɪvərɪ/ adj. 美味的
nouvelle cuisine /nuːˈvel kwɪˈziːn/ 新式烹调

The term European cuisine, when used by Westerners, refers to the cuisine in Europe. In this context people often use the word continental cuisine, especially in British English. Western European culinary delights are very diverse by themselves; however, there are common characteristics that distinguish them from cuisines of Asian countries.

If we compare the Western European cooking with traditional cooking of Asian countries we shall find out that meat is more prominent and substantial in the serving-sizes. Steak in particular is a common dish across the West. Western chefs usually have a far more in-depth knowledge concerning specific methods of preparing and serving the different cuts of meat than some Asian cooks. Western European cuisines also put significant emphasis on sauces as condiments, seasonings and their accompaniments. These foods use a lot of dairy products in the cooking process, except in nouvelle cuisine.

Wheat-flour bread is usually an important part of the cuisine and is the most common source of starch in them. They are usually in the form of pastas, dumplings and pastries, although the potato has become a major starch contributor. The taste of western European food is not limited to the Western Europe only; it has spread all across the globe. Consumers today have been exposed to a greater variety of cuisine and their tastes have changed markedly, with the result that flavor of the food has gained greater preference over the health content of the food. Savory snacks and dairy desserts are being sought out by people in order to satisfy their taste buds.

Based on the above passage, decide whether the following statements are true or false. Write T for true and F for false.

1. _____ Western cuisines are so different that it is impossible to describe characteristics they

share.
2. _____ With steak as a typical example, meat in Western cuisine is usually cooked in larger pieces.
3. _____ Potatoes have become a more common source of starch than wheat-flour in Western cuisine.
4. _____ People today seem to care more about the taste of the food than the nutrition it provides.

Part Two   Working Staff
二、酒店员工

1 Listen to the job description of each one in the department, correct the mistakes and put the right ones in the blanks.

(1) Restaurant Reception Manager:

To report to Restaurant Manager.

To supervise the work of Restaurant Waiters and Waitresses.

To coordinate reservations, keep restaurant work journals, keep cash flow, arrange seats and deal with guests' correspondences and inquiries.

a. _____

b. _____

中文提示：

　　餐厅接待经理：向餐厅经理汇报，负责管理餐厅服务员；协调客人的预订，写餐厅工作日志，收取订金，安排桌位，处理客人的来函和咨询。

(2) Headwaiter:

To report to Restaurant Manager, assisting the work of Restaurant Manager.

To supervise daily duties of busboys and busgirls.

To receive and greet guests.

To be in charge of taking orders.

To monitor service procedures.

a. _____

b. _____

中文提示：

　　餐厅领班：向餐厅经理汇报，协助餐厅经理的工作；监督勤杂工的日常工作；迎接和招待客人；负责为客人点菜；监督服务质量。

(3) Restaurant Cashier:

To handle guests' bills and cash and money exchange.

To tabulate data regarding bills, total amounts, dinning expenses in cash; register or record them in computers.

He or she may assist the wait staff with reservation or other various tasks.

a. _____

b. _____

中文提示：

餐厅收银员：处理客人账单以及现金交易；当天账单、现金收入制表，并录入计算机；有空时也帮助服务员订座，或协助完成其他工作。

2 Listen again and discuss the job description of the post you wish to hold in your career.

Part Three　Video for the Hotel
三、酒店视频

Table Taboos for Western Cuisine 西餐餐桌上的禁忌

Words and Expressions

rude /ru:d/ *adj.* 无礼的
mingle /ˈmɪŋgl/ *v.* 混合
medication /ˌmedɪˈkeɪʃn/ *n.* 药物
hygiene /ˈhaɪdʒi:n/ *n.* 卫生
offensive /əˈfensɪv/ *adj.* 无礼的
navigate /ˈnævɪgeɪt/ *v.* 确定……的位置

facilitate /fəˈsɪlɪteɪt/ *v.* 促进；帮助
agenda /əˈdʒendə/ *n.* 日程
obtrusive /əbˈtru:sɪv/ *adj.* 冒失的
lipstick /ˈlɪpstɪk/ *n.* 口红
embarrassed /ɪmˈbærəst/ *adj.* 尴尬的
reflect /rɪˈflekt/ *v.* 反映；表明

A Watch the video twice, and decide whether the following statements are true or false according to the video.

1. _____ When you arrive at the table, and you've found your place, it's extremely rude to change place cards.
2. _____ Taking medicine at the table can be accepted when you feel uncomfortable.
3. _____ You can use a toothpick after meal, getting something off your teeth at the table.
4. _____ It is impolite to receive the call when you hear your cellphone ringing.
5. _____ On some business events, you may ask for a taste of someone else's food, but never take away doggy bags.

B Watch the video again, and answer the following questions.

1. What should you not do about the place card and why?
   _____.

2. How do your dining companions feel if you take medicines at table?
   _____.

3. What should you not do concerning hygiene?
   _____.

4. What are the speaker's suggestions on the use of the cell phone at the table?
   _____.

5. What are the last things that may damage your image according to the speaker?
   _____.

Part Four　Dialogues in the Hotel
四、酒店对话

Scenario 1

Taking Orders 点菜

A Listen to Dialogue 1, and complete the following conversation with what you hear.

Waitress (W): Can I take your order now, sir?
Jason: Yes, please.
W: What (1) _____ would you like, sir?
Jason: What will you have to start, darling?
Jane: Mm, I'm not sure. I can't decide between the (2) _____ and the avocado and prawn salad. What about you?
Jason: Um, I'm going to have the stuffed mushrooms.
Jane: Well, if you're having the mushrooms, I'll have the avocado and (3) _____. I'll just steal some of your mushrooms!
W: So that's one stuffed mushrooms and one avocado and prawn salad. And for the (4)_____?
Jason: I fancy the veal escalope. What about you, dear?
Jane: Mm. That sounds good. I'll join you.
W: What (5) _____ would you like with your veal, madam?
Jane: Um, I'll have duchess potatoes and (6) _____, I think.

W:	Certainly, madam. And you, sir?
Jason:	I'll have a green salad, and (7) _____, please.
W:	Would you like anything to drink with your meal, sir?
Jason:	I'm not sure. What do you think, dear? Half a bottle of wine?
Jane:	Yes, that would be nice.
Jason:	Half a bottle of (8) _____, then.
W:	Certainly, sir.

B Divide your class into groups of two or three students, and do the dialogue again.

Scenario 2

Serving Foods 上菜

A Listen to Dialogue 2 and write numbers in the blanks to show the correct order of the conversation.

_____. **Waiter (W):** I'm sorry, madam. I'll get to check with our chef and the headwaiter.
(Minutes later, the waiter comes back.)

_____. **W:** I'm awfully sorry for giving you the wrong dish. I'll change it immediately and it will take about 15 minutes. Would you like to have some complimentary drink while waiting?

_____. **W:** Thank you for telling us. I assure you it won't happen again. And I hope you have a good time in our hotel.

_____. **W:** Your stuffed mushrooms. Please enjoy your meal.

_____. **Jane (J):** All right. Please get me some orange juice.
(Fifteen minutes later.)

_____. **J:** I'm afraid there is a mistake. I ordered the avocado and prawn salad.

_____. **W:** Sorry to have kept you waiting. Here is the avocado and prawn salad you ordered. You can try it and it's all on the house.

_____. **J:** That's good. Thank you very much.

B Role play: One student plays the role of waiter while another plays the role of Jane.

Scenario 3

American Breakfast 美式早餐

A Listen to Dialogue 3 and fill in the table with correct information.

Name of guest	Main course for breakfast	Juice preferred	Coffee preferred	Reservation (Yes) or (No)

B Listen to the dialogue again, and do a situational dialogue with your partner.

Waiter (W): Good morning. Can I help you?

Liu (L): I want to take a table.

W: Have you got a reservation?

L: Yes. I booked yesterday afternoon.

W: Oh, I know, you are Miss Liu.

L: Yes.

W: Now anything else?

L: I want an American breakfast with fried eggs, sunny side up.

W: What kind of juice do you prefer, madam?

L: Grapefruit juice and please make my coffee very strong.

W: Yes, madam. American breakfast with fried eggs, sunny side up, grapefruit juice and a black coffee. Am I right?

L: Yes, that's right.

W: Is there anything else, madam?

L: No, that's all.

Scenario 4

Change of the Food 换餐

A Listen to Dialogue 4 and choose True or False for the following sentences.

1. _____ The table has been reserved for three people.
2. _____ The waiter recommended veal escalope and duchess potatoes for the guests.
3. _____ According to the waiter's recommendation, they accepted his offer.
4. _____ They began with mushroom soup and then, were served by some seafood and chips.
5. _____ They accepted the wrong dishes because they were offered something free: a

bottle of beer.

B Listen to the dialogue again and answer the following questions.

1. How many guests came to have the food in the restaurant?

2. What foods did the waiter recommend to the guests?

3. What did they begin with their meal?

4. Did they order the dessert? Did they have any drinks?

Guest (G): Waiter, a table for two, please.
Waiter (W): Yes, this way please.
G: Can we see the menu, please?
W: Here you are.
G: What's good today?
W: I recommend veal escalope and duchess potatoes.
G: We don't want that. Well, perhaps we'll begin with mushroom soup, and follow by the Fricasseed Veal and Barbecued Spare Ribs.
W: Do you want any dessert?
G: No dessert, thanks. We'd like to have a bottle of Rum.
W: OK, thank you. Just for a moment.
(Fifteen minutes later)
W: Here is your order: the veal escalope, duchess potatoes and a bottle of Rum.
G: I'm afraid there is a mistake in the menu. We haven't ordered any veal escalope and duchess potatoes.
W: I'm sorry for giving you the wrong dish. I'll change it immediately. Would you like some complimentary drinks?
G: A bottle of beer, please.
W: Wait a moment. I'll be back right away.
G: Okay.

Additional Exercises:

Divide the class into groups. Each group makes a situational dialogue using words or phrases for Western Foods. You may refer to the working procedures or sentence patterns in Dialogue 1, Dialogue 2, Dialogue 3 and Dialogue 4.

Additional Words and Phrases 更多的词汇短语储备

西餐英文菜名

汤类

Cream of Mushroom Soup 奶油蘑菇汤
French Onion Soup 法式洋葱汤
Oxtail Soup 香浓牛尾汤
Hearty Lentil Soup 蔬菜干豆汤
Chilled Avocado Soup 牛油梨冻汤
Gazpacho 西班牙番茄冻汤

禽类

Braised Goose Liver in Red Wine 红酒鹅肝
Chicken Cordon Bleu 奶酪火腿鸡排
Braised Chicken with Red Wine 红酒烩鸡
Roast Stuffed Turkey 烤瓤火鸡
Barbecued Chicken Leg 烧烤鸡腿
Char-Grilled Chicken Breast 扒鸡胸

牛肉类

Stewed Beef 红烩牛肉
Fricasseed Veal 白烩小牛肉
T-Bone Steak T骨牛扒
Beef Stroganoff 俄式牛柳丝
Braised Ox-Tongue 烩牛舌
Osso Bucco 红烩牛膝

猪肉类

Barbecued Spare Ribs 烧烤排骨
Smoked Spare Ribs with Honey 烟熏蜜汁肋排
Pork Piccatta 意大利米兰猪排
Stuffed Poke Roulade with Yellow Peach Sauce 瓤馅猪肉卷配黄桃汁
Pan-fried Swiss Meat Loaf with Pesto Sauce 煎面包肠配香草汁
Deep-Fried Pork Chop 炸猪排

Part Five Consolidation
五、巩固练习

A Match the terms in column A with the definitions in column B.

A	B
1. to bake	A. to cook food in an oven using dry heat, with very little fat
2. to blanch	B. to cook food in a flavorful liquid slowly and for a long time
3. to boil	C. to cook food, usu. large pieces of solid food in an oven with fat
4. to poach	D. to cook food in a liquid just below boiling point
5. to roast	E. to cook in steam
6. to sauté	F. to cook food in a liquid either at or brought to boiling point
7. to steam	G. to cook in fat or oil over relatively high heat
8. to stew	H. to cook briefly in boiling water

B Translation

i. Translate the following sentences into Chinese.

1. Western European culinary (烹饪的) delights are very diverse by themselves; however, there are common characteristics that distinguish them from cuisines of Asian countries.
2. The Western restaurant is not only the place for supplying food, but the place for leisure, banquet (宴会) and communication.
3. We reserved (预订) a table for two at 7:00 in the name of Jason Smith. We want to be served in Western style.
4. Oh, any chance of a private room (包间)? It's my daughter's birthday, and I want it to be a celebration.
5. What would you have for your appetizer, something like hors d'oeuvres (餐前开胃小吃)? That would be on the house, of course.

ii. Translate the following sentences into English.

1. 中餐先上(begin with)冷盘,而西餐先上汤。
2. 西餐讲究各种原料所含卡路里(calories)和营养成分(nutrients)的合理搭配。
3. 西餐的原料(raw material)和烹饪方法(cooking methods)与中餐的有很大不同。
4. 贵店的招牌菜(house-special)是什么?
5. 不客气。服务员会马上为您点酒(take drink order)。

C Writing

A menu is the visible part of a hotel restaurant. Different restaurants offer different cuisines, customs and price ranges as well as different menu styles. There are menus of different types in a hotel restaurant and the most common type of menu is the static menu. The benefits of a static menu include increased familiarity among guests, dish stability across different locations and speedy production.

Suppose you're the manager of Food & Beverage Department, write a menu of Western foods, including the following categories of foods, each of which covers at least four dishes except soup.

Outline:

1. Name of the food
2. The price for each food
3. The chef's recommendation
4. Categories of food: (1)Beef; (2)Pork; (3)Poultry; (4)Soup

Notice: You may refer to Appendix 3 when you write the menu of Western foods.

Chapter 9
Western Beverage
西餐酒水

Major Topics   一、酒店知识：Alcohols and Beverages Offered by a Hotel 酒店提供的酒水
　　　　　　　　　二、酒店员工：Beverage Manager 酒水部经理
　　　　　　　　　　　　　　　　Sommelier 斟酒服务员（酒侍）
　　　　　　　　　　　　　　　　Bar Cashier 酒吧收银员
　　　　　　　　　三、酒店视频：How to Make a Mojito Cocktail? 如何调制莫吉托鸡尾酒？
　　　　　　　　　四、酒店对话：Scenario 1: Recommending Drinks 推荐酒水
　　　　　　　　　　　　　　　　Scenario 2: Ordering Wine 为客人点酒
　　　　　　　　　　　　　　　　Scenario 3: Explaining Drinks Mixing 介绍调酒方法
　　　　　　　　　　　　　　　　Scenario 4: Paying the Bill 付账
　　　　　　　　　五、巩固练习

> This chapter deals with the topic of Western beverages in the hotel restaurant. In *Part One*, you'll read ABC about alcohols and beverages offered by a hotel as a warming-up exercise. In *Part Two*, job description of working staff is provided for you to have some basics about the responsibility of each job in the Western restaurant. In *Part Three*, you'll watch a short video about how to make a mojito cocktail. In the next section, *Part Four* will provide some situational dialogues for you to practice some skills of beverage service in the bar based on different scenarios. *Part Five* includes other optional exercises to enhance your knowledge and skills of beverage service.

Part One ABC for Hotel
一、酒店知识

Alcohols and Beverages Offered by a Hotel 酒店提供的酒水

Word Tips

ingredient /ɪnˈɡriːdɪənt/ n. 材料；作料	concoction /kənˈkɒkʃn/ n. 调制
gin /dʒɪn/ n. 杜松子酒	rye /raɪ/ n. 裸麦威士忌酒
rum /rʌm/ n. 朗姆酒	sherry /ˈʃerɪ/ n. 雪利酒
vermouth /ˈvɜːməθ, ˈvɜːmuːθ/ n. 味美思酒	appetite /ˈæpɪtaɪt/ n. 食欲
ginger /ˈdʒɪndʒə(r)/ n. 生姜	ale /eɪl/ n. 麦芽酒
sommelier /səˈmelɪeɪ/ n. 斟酒服务员	steward /ˈstjuːəd/ n. 酒保

In hotel restaurants where alcoholic beverages are part of the meal services, they can be grouped into three categories: before-dinner, with dinner, and after-dinner drinks. The most common before-dinner drink is the cocktail, a concoction of liquor (such as gin, rye, and rum which are 80 to 100 proof) and ingredients such as bitters, fruit juices, ice, and fruit. Some before-dinner drinks are unmixed, such as vermouth and sherry; these are usually called aperitifs after the French term meaning to stimulate the appetite.

Drinks served with the meal are usually wine and beer. The customer makes a choice from a wine list, a menu of wines offered by the restaurant, listing the types and vintages. Some restaurants that are particularly luxurious employ a wine steward or sommelier who has information about the wines to serve them.

Liqueurs are served after dinner. They are usually strong and sweet such as Cointreau, Chartreuse, and Drambuie. They are sometimes called digestifs after the French word meaning an aid to digestion.

In addition to alcoholic drinks restaurants serve many kinds of non-alcoholic beverages. They vary according to the meal, with coffee or tea and fruit juices customary at breakfast, soft drinks, tea, and coffee at lunch, and coffee or tea at dinner. Coffee is often served first at breakfast, even before the customer's order is taken; at other meals it is served last unless the customer specifies differently. Iced tea and coffee are popular drinks in hot weather. Almost all restaurants have milk and soft drinks such as colas and ginger ale.

A special note should be made about water. In the United States it is customary for the waiter to pour iced water for the guests as soon as they are seated, but this is not the usual practice in many other countries. In some, water is not served at all; in others it is not iced; and in still others, a different beverage is served, such as tea in China and Japan.

Based on the above passage, decide whether the following statements are true or false. Write T for true and F for false.

1. _____ In Western restaurants cocktails are usually served before the meal to stimulate the appetite.
2. _____ A digestif, a term which comes from French, refers to a beverage served at the end of a meal to help digest food.
3. _____ According to the passage, coffee can be served at all meals of the day.
4. _____ It is a common practice across the world to serve iced water when guests are seated in a restaurant.

Part Two Working Staff
二、酒店员工

1 Listen to the job description of each one in the department, correct the mistakes and put the right ones in the blanks.

(1) **Beverage Manager** reports straight to Food and Beverage Manager, oversees the purchase and supply of beverages. Main obligations are:

To update the beverage list.
To watch the beverage market, dealing with drinks selections and pricing.
To maintain and control the stock of beverage.
To direct and supervise employees working with beverages.
To promote liquors and wines.
　a. _____
　b. _____
中文提示：
　　酒水部经理：直接向餐饮部经理汇报，监督饮料销售和供应。主要职责有更新饮料供应清单掌握饮料市场动态，选购饮料和定价，保持和控制饮料库存，指导和监督酒水部员工工作，负责饮料促销。

(2) **Sommelier** reports to Head Bartender; aids the Head Bartender with his work. The main obligations are:

To mix and deliver beverage.
To keep the bar sanitary and clean.
　a. _____
　b. _____
中文提示：
　　斟酒服务员（酒侍）：向酒吧领班汇报，协助领班工作，为客人调酒、送酒，帮助整理库存和清理酒吧。

(3) **Bar Cashier**

A busy bar may hire a bar cahier, but this job is usually taken by bartenders. A separate bar cashier can help enhance the efficiency of bar operations. The main obligations are:

To report to Bar Manager/Supervisor.

To prepare bills and receipts, handle small changes.

To control cash flow and credit card transactions.

a. _____

b. _____

中文提示：

酒吧收银员：生意好的酒吧可能会雇用一名专职的酒吧收银员，但这项工作通常是酒吧招待来担任。酒吧收银员向酒吧经理或主任汇报，为客人准备账单，收款、开票，监控现金和信用卡交易。

2 Listen again and discuss the job description of the post you wish to hold in your career.

Part Three　Video for the Hotel
三、酒店视频

How to Make a Mojito Cocktail? 如何调制莫吉托鸡尾酒？

Word Tips

pint /paɪnt/ n. 品脱(液体或者干量名)　　muddle /ˈmʌdl/ v. 使混合
dash /dæʃ/ n. 注入(少量)　　　　　　　　muddler /ˈmʌdlə/ n. 搅拌器
mint /mɪnt/ n. 薄荷　　　　　　　　　　　lime /laɪm/ n. 酸橙
sprig /sprɪg/ n. 小枝,条　　　　　　　　　garnish /ˈɡɑːnɪʃ/ v. 装饰

A Watch the video twice, and decide whether the following statements are true or false according to the video.

1. _____ This is a really popular drink, especially in the winters.
2. _____ So firstly, the waiter is going to fill the glass up, just a little bit, with ice.
3. _____ And the waiter is probably going to want to pick off, maybe five or six, even seven bits of lime, of bits of mint.
4. _____ The ingredients for this drink are going to be about 2 ounces of rum, of a light rum.

5. _____ Press the lime at the bottom of the glass so that the flavors will come out.

B Watch the video again, and answer the following questions.

1. Are any containers used to make a Mojito?
   _____.

2. How many steps are there to make a Mojito professionally?
   _____.

3. What is the people's opinion about the Mojito?
   _____.

4. How can we make the flavors come out?
   _____.

5. What is your opinion of being a professional mixer?
   _____.

Part Four Dialogues in the Hotel
四、酒店对话

Scenario 1

Recommending Drinks 推荐酒水

A Listen to Dialogue 1 and choose True or False for the following sentences.
1. _____ The waiter recommended a Barsac that goes well with the pan-fried white fish fillet.
2. _____ Then the waiter recommended Chateau Haut Lafite.
3. _____ Jason did not accept the waiter's advice and choose another kind of wines.
4. _____ Chateau Haut Lafite should be used to go well with T-bone.
5. _____ Jane and Jason picked up Crème de Cassis to complete their meal in three kinds of liquors, Crème de Cassis, Cointreau, or Triple Sec.

B Listen to the dialogue and answer the following questions.
1. How many guests come to have the wines in the restaurant?
   _____

2. How many kinds of wines are mentioned in the conversation?
   _____

3. Which kind of wine is used to go well with the pan-fried white fish fillet?
   _____

4. At last, how many kinds of liqueurs are ordered to complete their meal?

Waiter (W): What wine would you like to have with your dinner?
Jane: You have such an extensive cellar. What vintage can you recommend?
W: (*To Jane*) Well, I think a Barsac goes very well with your pan-fried white fish fillet.
Jane: OK. A half bottle of it.
W: Yes, madam. (*To the gentleman*) Sir, I'd recommend Chateau Haut Lafite for your T-bone.
Jason: Good. A half bottle of it, too.
W: Would you like a liqueur to complete your meal?
Jason: What do you have?
W: What about Crème de Cassis, Cointreau, or Triple Sec?
Jason: Just Cointreau, please.
(*The wine waiter repeats the order.*)
W: Please wait a moment.

Scenario 2

Ordering Wine 为客人点酒

A Listen to Dialogue 2 and fill in the table with correct information.

Name of wines or liquors	Wine or liquor preferred	Alcoholic or none-alcoholic	On the rocks or straight

B Listen to the dialogue again, and do a situational dialogue with your partner.

A: Hello, sir. What can I do for you?
B: I would like to have a drink.
A: Here is the wine list. We have the brandy, whisky, rum and some soft wine. Which would you prefer?
B: Which one is with a little alcoholic?
A: Brandy.
B: OK.
B: Need I put ice in it?

A: Oh, no. Just the brandy.
B: OK. Wait for a moment, sir.

Scenario 3

Explaining Drinks Mixing 介绍调酒方法

A Listen to Dialogue 3, and complete the following conversation with what you hear.

Guest(G): Do you know how to make a Singapore Sundown?
Bartender(B): Uh, no. I'm afraid I don't. But if you would like to tell me, I'd be happy to (1) _____. What's in it, sir?
G: Uh, brandy, crème de cacao and (2) _____.
B: Mm. That sounds nice. So, we pour one measure of brandy and add another measure of crème de cacao and (3) _____ and then finally (4) _____ champagne. Is that it, sir?
G: That sounds right. But the champagne must be very cold, and it's served in a (5) _____.
B: Right, sir. I'll have your Singapore Sundown ready (6) _____.
G: Thank you.

B Divide your class into groups of two or three students, and do the dialogue again.

Scenario 4

Paying the Bill 付账

A Listen to Dialogue 4 and write numbers in the blanks to show the correct order of the conversation.

_____. **G (Guest):** No, thank you. Can we have the bill, please?
_____. **W: (Waiter):** Are you staying at the hotel?
_____. **G:** Do you take credit cards or shall I pay in cash?
_____. **W:** Could I bring you anything else?
_____. **G:** Sure... There you go.
_____. **W:** May I see your room card, please?
_____. **G:** Yes, I am.
_____. **W:** Thank you, sir.
_____. **W:** Since you are staying at the hotel, we can put it on your hotel bill. The hotel will charge you when you leave.
_____. **G:** That's good.
_____. **W:** Yes, sir. Just a moment. (*Handing the bill to the guest*) Here it is. Please check it.

B Role play: One student plays the role of waiter while another plays the role of the guest.

Additional Exercises:

Divide the class into groups. Each group makes a situational dialogue using words or phrases for the Western beverages. You may refer to the working procedures or sentence patterns in Dialogue 1, Dialogue 2, Dialogue 3 and Dialogue 4.

Additional Words and Phrases 更多的词汇短语储备

Word Tips

Brandy 白兰地	Remy Martin 人头马
Hennessy 轩尼诗	Remy Martin Lovis 路易十三
Dewar's 德华士	Singleton 苏格兰威
Four Roses 四玫瑰	Old Parr 老伯威

Part Five   Consolidation
五、巩固练习

A Read the following the passage carefully and complete the cloze exercise after the text.

Types of Wine 葡萄酒的种类

Choosing the right type of wine depends on numerous factors—personal preferences, the food you're pairing it with and budget, among others. The (1) _____ number of types of wine can be overwhelming as you're searching for something to bring home for dinner, (2) _____ with a little information on the types of wine available, you can make your search easy and fruitful.

Red Wines

Red wines are characterized by their rich, dark red color and heavy, complex (3)_____. Red wines are often described (4) _____ hearty and bold tasting. Red wines are generally (5) _____ with red meat or heavy pasta dishes. Examples of some commonly served red wines include Beaujolais, Chianti, Cabernet Sauvignon, Pinot Noir, Merlot and Zinfandel.

White Wines
White wines are generally sweeter and lighter than red wines. They have a (6)_____ complex flavor profile than red wines, can be dry or sweet, and often contain (7)_____ of fruits and citrus. White wines are characterized by their light golden yellow tone. Some (8)_____ types of white wine include Chardonnay, Pinot Grigio, Pinot Gris, Riesling and Sauvignon Blanc. White wines are generally paired with light dishes, such as fish and salads.

Dessert Wines
Dessert wines are so (9)_____ because they're sweeter than red or white wines and made to be paired with desserts or other sweet foods. Dessert wines are made either through added sugar content, (10)_____ harvesting the grapes late when they have high levels of sugar, (11)_____ by drying grapes to concentrate the sugars. Dessert wines can be either white or red. The most commonly served type of dessert wine is Port, a rich, dark, sweet red wine.

Sparkling Wines
Sparkling wines are wines that contain (12)_____ carbon dioxide. Sparkling wines are generally dry and sweet, and have a light golden, nearly clear tone.

(13)_____, sparkling wines are served at celebrations and (14)_____ special occasions. (15)_____ Champagne is the best known of the sparkling wines, some other common types of sparkling wines are Cava, Crémant d'Alsace, Moscato d'Asti and Prosecco.

1. A. sheer   B. only   C. pure   D. fine
2. A. or   B. as   C. but   D. for
3. A. favor   B. savor   C. cellar   D. flavor
4. A. by   B. of   C. like   D. as
5. A. parted   B. paired   C. chilled   D. cooked
6. A. less   B. greater   C. fewer   D. more
7. A. seeds   B. notes   C. shapes   D. colors
8. A. usual   B. normal   C. common   D. customary
9. A. named   B. referred   C. told   D. stated
10. A. after   B. on   C. by   D. till
11. A. and   B. or else   C. or   D. nor
12. A. creating bubble   B. bubble created
    C. created bubble   D. bubble creating
13. A. In general B. As usual   C. Altogether   D. Above all
14. A. in case of B. in honor of   C. in spite of   D. on behalf of
15. A. But   B. Although   C. Despite   D. However

B Translation

i. Translate the following sentences into Chinese.

1. Some restaurants that are particularly luxurious employ a wine steward (斟酒服务员) or sommelier who has information about the wines to serve guests.
2. In addition to alcoholic drinks restaurants serve many kinds of non-alcoholic (不含酒精) beverages.
3. You need to understand how to use these three elements to produce a professionally made cocktail (鸡尾酒).
4. Cocktails have become the must-have (必需) item on any bar menu.
5. Almost all restaurants have milk and soft drinks (软饮料) such as colas, orange juice.

ii. Translate the following sentences into English.

1. 很抱歉先生,我们暂时没有这种酒。我建议您试一杯玛莉咖啡酒(Tia Maria)。
2. 餐中酒饮料通常用(serve with)葡萄酒和啤酒。
3. 我们酒的储量很大(extensive)。请先看酒单(drink list)。
4. 不成熟的葡萄酿出轻质(lighter bodied)葡萄酒。你要哪一种葡萄酒?
5. 鸡尾酒现在是一种时尚(fashion),最起码也是时尚的标志。

C Writing

Drink List 酒水单

You can mix wine and hard liquor into a wide variety of flavorful cocktails. Mixed drinks are beverages containing two or more ingredients. They can be alcoholic, based on a certain type of spirit with added juices, other alcoholic beverages, fruits or garnish, or alcohol-free. Bartenders in the hotel combine almost everything behind the bar to give you new and original drinks.

The hotel bar has an extensive cellar of the wines. Suppose you're the manager of Foods and Beverage Department, write a drink list of cocktails for a party which will be held in the bar. The following cocktails are the musts of the wine list because they have been ordered by the host.

- Bloody Mary 血腥玛丽
- Rum and Cola 朗姆可乐
- Margarita 玛格丽特鸡尾酒
- Screwdriver 螺丝钻
- Bourbon and Cola 波旁可乐

Outline:

1. Name of the wines or liquors
2. The price for each wine or liquor
3. The chef's recommendation
4. The drinks on the house

Notice: You may refer to Appendix 4 when you write the drink list.

Chapter 10
Chinese Food
中式餐点

Major Topics
一、酒店知识：Chinese Cuisine 中国菜
二、酒店员工：Restaurant Manager 餐厅经理
　　　　　　　Waiter/Waitress 服务员
　　　　　　　Busser 餐馆勤杂工
　　　　　　　Executive Chef (Chef de cuisine) 厨师长
三、酒店视频：Chinese Dining and Serving Etiquette 中餐上菜服务礼仪
四、酒店对话：Scenario 1: Reservation for a Table 订座
　　　　　　　Scenario 2: Recommendation of Chinese Dishes 推荐中国菜
　　　　　　　Scenario 3: Taking Orders 点菜
　　　　　　　Scenario 4: Chinese Breakfast 中式早餐
五、巩固练习

　　This chapter centers on the topic of serving Chinese food in the hotel restaurant. In *Part One*, you'll read ABC about Chinese cuisine as a warming-up exercise. In *Part Two*, job description of working staff is provided for you to have some basics about the responsibility of each job at a Chinese restaurant. In *Part Three*, you'll watch a short video about Chinese dining and serving etiquette. In the next section, *Part Four* will provide some situational dialogues for you to practice the Chinese food service based on different scenarios. *Part Five* includes additional exercises to enhance your knowledge and skills of dining or working in a restaurant, and get to know how to eat Chinese food in a healthy way.

Part One ABC for Hotel
一、酒店知识

Chinese Cuisine 中国菜

Word Tips

characteristic /ˌkærəktəˈrɪstɪk/ adj. 典型的；特有的
numerous /ˈnjuːmərəs/ a. 许多的，大批的
aromatic /ˌærəˈmætɪk/ adj. 芳香的，香味的
exquisite /ɪkˈskwɪzɪt/ adj. 精致的，精巧的
braise /breɪz/ v. (用文火)炖，焖(肉)
prevalent /ˈprevələnt/ adj. 行的，盛行的

lavish /ˈlævɪʃ/ adj. 过于丰富的，过度的
influential /ˌɪnfluˈenʃl/ adj. 有影响的
crispness /ˈkrɪspnəs/ n. 脆
pursue /pəˈsjuː/ v. 追求
specialty /ˈspeʃəltɪ/ n. 特色菜，新出品
numb /nʌm/ v. 使麻木

In China, different geography, climate, resources, produce and food habits combine to form characteristic local cuisines, namely, the "four flavors" and "eight regional cuisines." The "four flavors" refer to those of Shandong, Sichuan, Guangdong and Huaiyang (Yangzhou). The "eight regional cuisines" refer to the local modifications of the "four flavors," including Shandong Cuisine, Sichuan Cuisine, Hunan Cuisine, Guangdong Cuisine, Fujian Cuisine, Jiangsu Cuisine, Zhejiang Cuisine and Anhui Cuisine. From the dishes served at family meals to lavish banquets, local famous foods are too numerous to list, and the delicious foods of all kinds of taste reflect the highly developed tradition of food culture and the characteristic regional cultures of China.

Lu Cuisine is one of the most influential and popular cuisines in China. "Lu" is short for Shandong Province, which is one of the cradles of Chinese ancient culture. Shandong Cuisine emphasizes purity of the seasonings and is a little salty. It features freshness, tenderness, aroma and crispness. There are over 30 kinds of common cooking techniques, of which, "bao (quick stir-frying), chao (frying), shao (stewing), ta (boiling) and pa (braising)" are outstanding. As the first cuisine of north China, many basic courses of high-class feasts prepared for festivals and birthdays were developed based on Shandong cuisine. It also had an important influence on the formation of the local cuisines of Beijing, Tianjin and northeast China. Yellow River Fish and Dezhou Stewed Chicken are two popular dishes of Lu Cuisine.

Sichuan Cuisine is a local cuisine that developed in early times, forming part of the culture of ancient Sichuan in Southwestern China. Now, Sichuan Cuisine is widely enjoyed all over China and has spread to many countries. Mention Sichuan Cuisine and tongue-numbing and spicy tastes come to mind. Seasonings are very important in Sichuan Cuisine and many different flavors abound. If the cook is skillful enough, seven flavors—sour, sweet, bitter, spicy, tongue-numbing, aromatic and salty should be detected. Most Sichuan dishes are economic and flavorful home style ones, simple and fresh. Mapo Tofu, Pork Slivers in Fish-flavor Sauce, and Twice-cooked Pork are traditional flavorful dishes.

Yue Cuisine refers to that of Guangdong Province, mainly composed of the flavors of Guangzhou, Chaozhou and Dongjiang and best represented by that of Guangzhou. It has a unique "southland" flavor and is famous for the rare and exquisite ingredients and varied recipes to suit the tastes of the eaters. Guangdong Cuisine stresses exquisite preparation and provides enjoyment with delicate, well-chosen ingredients and beautiful presentation. It has strict requirements in regard to ingredients, cutting skill, cooking duration, tableware, serving style and so on. It pursues the whole effect of the dishes — color, fragrance, taste and shape. Sliced Boiled Chicken, Soup of the Day and Braised Shark Fin in Brown Sauce are the traditional dishes of Guangdong Cuisine.

Huaiyang Cuisine, composed of Huai'an, Yangzhou, Nanjing, Suzhou and Zhejiang Cuisines, with many ingredients but mainly river, lake and sea foods. The cutting skill is exquisite and the cooking methods are varied — braising, stewing, simmering and warming. Care is taken to preserve the original flavor of the ingredients, light, fresh, as well as salty with a little sweetness. The dishes are elegant and beautiful in form and quality. Squirrel-like Mandarin Fish, Tofu Boiled in Chicken Broth are specialties of Yangzhou style.

Dishes in these major cuisines in China are characterized by diversified cooking skills, with each having its strong points. Being prevalent across China, dishes of different styles have been adding rich flavors into people's diet, which also reflect the important role of diet in the Chinese life.

Based on the above passage, decide whether the following statements are true or false. Write T for true and F for false.

1. _____ According to the passage, food habits are the most important factor in the formation of a local cuisine.
2. _____ Shandong cuisine borrowed much from the local cuisine of Beijing when developing its own characteristics.
3. _____ What makes Sichuan cuisine special is that the dishes are always cooked with tongue-numbing and spicy flavors.
4. _____ Based on the passage, we can see that Yue Cuisine, Huaiyang Cuisine pay attention to both how the dishes taste and what the dishes look like.

Part Two　Working Staff
二、酒店员工

1 Listen to the job description of each one in the department, correct the mistakes and put the right ones in the blanks.

(1) **Restaurant Manager**

Restaurant Manager reports to Food and Beverage Manager, taking charge of daily operations of the restaurant. His major responsibilities are:

To regulate business operations.

To resolve customer issues.

To schedule the staff.

To monitor and evaluate employee attitudes.

To train staff.

To monitor inventory (ordering/ delivery).

To meet health and safety regulations.

a. _____

b. _____

中文提示：

餐厅经理：向餐饮部经理汇报，主管餐厅的日常工作，管理餐厅经营活动，处理顾客投诉，分配员工工作，监管考评员工，培训员工，管理库存（采购和交付），确保卫生和安全条例的有效执行。

(2) **Waiter/Waitress**

Waiting staff are those who work at a restaurant or a bar attending customers—supplying them with food and drink as requested. The duties of wait staff include:

To prepare tables for a meal.

To take customers' notes.

To serve drinks and food.

To clean up before, after and during meals.

a. _____

b. _____

中文提示：

服务员：指在餐馆或酒吧工作，向顾客提供菜品和饮料的服人员，其主要职责有：布置餐桌；为客人点菜；上菜、上饮料；上菜前后和客人就餐时清洁餐桌，保持整洁。

(3) **Busser**

Busser, also called "busboy" or "busgirl" are terms used in the United States for someone who works in the catering industry. The duties of a busser include:

To clear tables.

To take used dishes to the dishwasher.

To assist the wait staff.

A busser's duties generally depend on the size of the restaurant. In large restaurants with many employees, a busser may not be required to do much in the kitchen except bring in dirty dishes and items from the dining hall. In small restaurants with a few employees, they may have additional duties, like washing dishes, storing the kitchen, taking out the trash, etc.

a. _____

b. _____

中文提示：

餐馆勤杂工：也叫"busboy"或"busgirl"，是美国人对餐饮业服务人员的称谓，其主要职责有清洁餐桌，将用过的餐具送到洗碟机清洗，协助服务员完成其他工作。勤杂工职责范围取决于餐馆大小。在雇佣员工多的大餐馆，餐馆勤杂工除了将用过的餐具从餐厅送到厨房外，不会被要求做其他后厨工作；在雇佣员工少的小餐馆，餐馆勤杂工还要做其他工作，如洗碗、进货、清运垃圾等。

(4) Executive Chef (Chef de cuisine)

In some establishments, the Executive Chef may report to the Food and Beverage Manager. He is responsible for entire kitchen operations, and his major responsibilities include:

To plan menu.

To control cost.

To train the bussers.

To schedule the kitchen staff.

To maintain food safety and cooking standards.

a. _____

b. _____

中文提示：

厨师长：在某些公司，厨师长向餐饮部经理汇报，负责整个厨房工作的运行和管理，其主要职责包括编制菜单，控制成本，培训厨房员工，安排班组任务，确保食品安全、保证烹饪标准。

2 Listen again and discuss the job description of the post you wish to hold in your career.

Part Three Video for the Hotel
三、酒店视频

Chinese Dining and Serving Etiquette 中餐上菜服务礼仪

Word Tips

generous /ˈdʒenərəs/ *adj.* 慷慨的，大度的
anxious /ˈæŋkʃəs/ *adj.* 焦虑的；担忧的
offer /ˈɒfə(r)/ *v.* 提议，建议
bring out 端出来，上菜

rank /ræŋk/ *n.* 等级；排位
stock /stɒk/ *v.* 囤积；办货
go in /ɡəʊ ɪn/ 进入，进去
yield to 让步于，顺从

A Watch the video twice, and decide whether the following statements are true or false according to the video.

1. _____ When you have a meal with Chinese, who takes the dish first is not actually very important.
2. _____ The Chinese would like to bring out all of the dishes together to treat the guests.
3. _____ The guest should not take a piece first. Instead, he or she should sit for a while, and wait until somebody more "important" or ranking higher comes.
4. _____ Often an elder person would give way or yield to a younger person to take that first piece of food.
5. _____ If you want to be polite in the Chinese society, you'd better take the last piece of food.

B Watch the video again, and answer the following questions.

1. What do the Chinese prefer? The food delivered together, or just one by one? Why?
   _____.

2. What are the differences between the family setting and the business setting in eating etiquette?
   _____.

3. What is the general rule to follow if a foreigner wishes to appear polite when dining with Chinese people?
   _____.

Part Four   Dialogues in the Hotel
四、酒店对话

Scenario 1

Reservation for a Table 订座

A Listen to Dialogue 1 and mark True or False for the following sentences.
1. _____ The couple is waiting to be seated in a crowded restaurant although they have a reservation in advance.
2. _____ They have to wait at the lounge for more than half an hour until a table is available.
3. _____ The guests may have a drink at the lounge while waiting for the table, but they refuse.
4. _____ The couple are guaranteed to have a table by the window when they come back.

B Listen to the dialogue again and answer the following questions.
1. How many guests come in to have the food and what's their relation?

2. Why aren't they seated at once?

3. How would the waiter arrange them and do they act as what he says?

4. Do they come back to the restaurant? What time is it?

Waiter (W): Do you have a reservation, sir?
Guest (G): No, I am afraid we don't.
W: I'm sorry. The restaurant is full now. You have to wait for about half an hour. Would you care to have a drink at the lounge until a table is available?
G: No, thanks. We'll come back later. May I reserve a table for two?
W: Yes, of course. May I have your name, sir?
G: Bruce. By the way, can we have a table by the window?
W: We'll try to arrange it but I can't guarantee, sir.
G: That's fine.(*Half an hour later, the couple come back.*)
W: Your table is ready, sir. Please step this way.

Scenario 2

Recommendation of Chinese Dishes 推荐中国菜

A Listen to Dialogue 2 and write numbers in the blanks to show the correct order of the conversation.

_____ **Waiter (W):** Huaiyang food is well-known for its cutting technique and original flavor. And Dried Bean Curd Shreds in Chicken Soup is many Huaiyang chefs' recommendation.

_____ **W:** Yes, most Sichuan dishes are hot and spicy, and they taste different.

_____ **W:** They are Shandong Cuisine, Guangdong Cuisine, Sichuan Cuisine, and Huaiyang Cuisine.

_____ **Jane (J):** I hear that there are many regional cuisines in China, aren't there?

_____ **W:** Well, it's a long story to tell. Briefly speaking, Shandong food is heavy but not greasy while Guangdong food is light and fresh. The famous specialties of these two are Roast Beijing Duck and Roast Sucking Pig.

_____ **J:** Oh? What are the main differences?

_____ **W:** Right you are. There are four major cuisines, or say, four styles.

_____ **J:** What are they?

_____ **J:** How about the Huaiyang food?

_____ **J:** People say that Sichuan cuisine is very hot, isn't it?

_____ **J:** Great! I'll be going there. Thank you for your information.

_____ **W:** I think Mapo Tofu and Pork Slivers in Fish-flavor Sauce are worth trying. Our Sichuan restaurant is on the third floor.

_____ **J:** Really? I like hot food. So what's your recommendation for me?

B Role play: One student plays the role of waiter while another plays the role of Jane.

Scenario 3

Taking Orders 点菜

Word Tips

Twice-cooked Pork 回锅肉   Mapo Tofu 麻婆豆腐
Sautéed Eggplant with Fish Flavor 鱼香茄子   jiaozi 饺子
Roast Beijing Duck 北京烤鸭   Roast Sucking Pig 烤乳猪
white wine 白葡萄酒   whisky 威士忌
Pork Slivers in Fish-flavor Sauce 鱼香肉丝
Dried Bean Curd Shreds in Chicken Soup 干豌豆瓣鸡汤

A Listen to Dialogue 3, and complete the following conversation with what you hear.

Waitress (W): Are you ready to order now, sir?

Jason (J): No, I'm still looking at (1) _____. We'd like to try some Sichuan food, something of home style.

W: Then you might want to have Twice-cooked Pork and Mapo Tofu. They are (2)_____.

J: Are they very spicy and hot? My wife does not like hot food very much.

W: No really. They are (3) _____ than many other Sichuan dishes.

J: OK. I'll have them.

W: Very well, sir. Would you like (4)_____ for your lunch?

J: Oh, yes. Could you make a suggestion for us?

W: Yes. How about Sautéed Eggplant with Fish Flavor? That is eggplant sautéed with (5) _____. It's our chef's dish.

J: That sounds good. I'll have a try.

W: Any Chinese staple food? Rice or (6) _____?

J: Just a bowl of rice, please.

W: Yes, sir. So, Twice-cooked Pork, Mapo Tofu, Sautéed Eggplant with Fish Flavor and (7) _____.

J: That's right.

W: Sir, your dishes will take 15 minutes to prepare. While waiting, would you like (8) _____?

J: Jasmine tea, please.

W: Certainly. Just a moment.

B Divide your class into groups of two or three students, and do the dialogue again.

Scenario 4

Chinese Breakfast 中式早餐

A Listen to Dialogue 4 and fill in the table with correct information.

Name of the learner	Some foods for Chinese breakfast	Suggestions on learning to cook	Final help

B Listen to the dialogue again, and do a situational dialogue with your partner.

Tom (T): Hi, May. Nice to meet you!
May (M): Hi, Tom. Do you know how to cook any Chinese dishes?
T: Yes, what dishes would you like to cook?
M: I'd like to make breakfast myself. Any suggestions?
T: Of course. There are various kinds of foods, such as sliced noodles, hand-pulled noodles, dumplings, fried dumplings, steamed buns, meat pies, fried noodles, fried rice, and wonton. Which one do you want?
M: Uh... so complicated, and I'm not sure. But they do make my mouth water. Ha-ha. I only want to learn how to make something simple.
T: OK, I can help. I'll give you a recipe soon and you could also search on the Internet.
M: I'm afraid the recipe will not help me that much and I couldn't understand it well.
T: Then, I'll go to your house and show you how to cook. And you'd better try them first.
M: Yeah, certainly I will and thank you very much!

Additional Exercises:

Divide the class into groups. Each group makes a situational dialogue using words or phrases for the Chinese Foods. You may refer to the working procedures or sentence patterns in Dialogue 1, Dialogue 2, Dialogue 3 and Dialogue 4.

Additional Words and Phrases 更多的词汇短语储备

Word Tips

冷菜类 Cold Dishes
白菜心拌蜇头：Marinated Jellyfish and Chinese Cabbage in Vinaigrette
白灵菇扣鸭掌：Mushrooms with Duck Feet
拌豆腐丝：Shredded Tofu with Sauce

热菜 Hot Dishes   猪肉类 Pork
白菜豆腐焖酥肉：Braised Pork Cubes with Tofu and Chinese Cabbage
鲍鱼红烧肉：Braised Pork with Abalone
鲍汁扣东坡肉：Braised Dongpo Pork with Abalone Sauce

牛肉类 Beef
XO酱炒牛柳条：Sautéed Beef Filet in XO Sauce
爆炒牛肋骨：Sautéed Beef Ribs
彩椒牛柳：Sautéed Beef Filet with Bell Peppers

Part Five Consolidation
五、巩固练习

A Identify the mistakes of translation in Chinese dishes and put the right ones in the table.

Names of Dishes	Mistranslated names	Correct names
童子鸡	Chicken Without Sex	
红烧狮子头	Red Burned Lion Head	
麻婆豆腐	Tofu Made by Woman with Freckles	
夫妻肺片	Husband and Wife's lung slice	
四喜丸子	Four Glad Meat Balls	
火爆腰花	Pork Flower	
木须肉	Wood Mustache Meat	
泡椒凤爪	Phoenix Paws with Pickled Peppers	
醉鸡	Drunken Chicken	
驴打滚儿	Donkey Rolling on the Ground	

B Translation

i. Translate the following sentences into Chinese.

1. In China, different geography, climate, resources, produce and food habits combine to form characteristic local cuisines, namely, the "four flavors（四大风味）" and "eight regional cuisines(八大菜系)."
2. Yue Cuisine(粤菜) has a unique "southland" flavor("南国"风味) and is famous for the rare and exquisite ingredients and varied recipes to suit the tastes of the eaters.
3. The origin of Chinese chopsticks is directly related to the emergence and development of primitive agriculture as well as to the invention and development of pottery ware(陶制器皿).
4. Some translations of Chinese dishes will prove entirely incomprehensible(不懂) while others will simply put you off your food(倒胃口).
5. Retain the pinyin(拼音) name for Chinese specialties(特色菜): instead of translating jiaozi generally as dumplings, the pinyin is used.

ii. Translate the following sentences into English.
1. 中国菜完全将颜色、形状、外观和味道融合(fusion)为一体。
2. 您可以点回锅肉和麻婆豆腐,这是我们的特色菜(specialty)。
3. 简单来说,山东菜口味重(heavy),而广东菜则较清淡新鲜(light and fresh)。
4. 淮阳菜以其刀工(cutting technique)精细和风味原始著称(be well-known)。
5. 在中国餐馆,最尊贵的位置(be positioned in)是面向门的地方。

iii. Translate at least 10 Chinese dishes according to examples given using the following cooking techniques.

steamed 蒸	shredded 切丝	boiled 煮
minced; chopped 切碎	fried 炸;煎	mashed 捣碎
ground 磨碎	smoked 熏	roast 烤
flavor 有风味的	stewed 炖	salty 咸的
braised 焖	simmered 煨	sautéed 煸
quick fried 爆	broiled 炙	instant-boiled 涮
marinated 浸泡	steamed in clear soup 清蒸	stewed in clear soup 清炖
skewered 串烤	sliced 切片	pickled 盐醋泡的

Examples
1. 南瓜香芋蒸排骨: Steamed Spare Ribs with Pumpkin and Taro
2. 拌豆腐丝: Shredded Tofu with Sauce
3. 海竹笙煮双鲜: Boiled Seafood with Bamboo Fungus
4. 蚂蚁上树: Sautéed Vermicelli with Spicy Minced Pork
5. 香椿煎蛋: Fried Eggs with Chopped Chinese Toon Leaves
6. 煎猪柳: Pan-Fried Pork Filet
7. 拌茄泥: Mashed Eggplant with Garlic
8. 炸酱面: Noodles with Ground Pork
9. 四川樟茶鸭: Smoked Duck, Sichuan Style
10. 北菇扒大鸭: Braised Duck with Black Mushrooms and Vegetables
11. 北京烤鸭: Beijing Roast Duck
12. 竹香鲫鱼: Fried Crucian Carp with Bamboo Flavour
13. 清蒸甲鱼: Steamed Turtle
14. 龙眼风味肠: Sausage Stuffed with Salty Eggs
15. 煎烹虾仁: Fried and Simmered Shrimps
16. 京酱肉丝: Sautéed Shredded Pork in Sweet Bean Sauce
17. 炝黄瓜: Quick-Fried Cucumber
18. 烤虾: Broiled Shrimp
19. 涮羊肉: Instant-boiled Mutton
20. 腌三文鱼: Marinated Salmon
21. 清蒸鱼: Steamed Fish in Clear Soup

22. 清炖猪蹄:	Stewed Pig Feet in Clear Soup
23. 串烧白鳝:	Skewered Eels
24. 酱爆鸭片:	Sautéed Sliced Duck in Soy Sauce
25. 跳水木耳:	Black Fungus with Pickled Capsicum

 Writing

Menu Pricing 菜品定价

An effective food menu is well-organized, descriptive and current. Arranging food selections by course will guide diners through the menu in chronological order. As the manager of a restaurant, one of the most important tasks you'll have is to set prices for the dishes offered on your menu. Your prices will determine your profit margin and impact the success of a restaurant.

Suppose you are the manager of a Chinese restaurant in a hotel, write a Chinese food menu, and set proper price for each item. There are a few things to consider when you price your restaurant menu.

Outline:

1. Divide your food cost by 35 percent. If the sandwich platter costs $2 to make, the calculation is as follows: 2/0.35, which equals $5.71. Always round up, which would make it $5.99.

2. Labor is usually about 25 percent of your sales, so use this as a guide to price your menu.

3. Overhead includes all costs not related to labor or food cost, like rent, utilities, advertising and supplies.

4. People are willing to pay more for ambiance. That same sandwich platter might cost $12 if you serve it on fine china with a fancy garnish.

Chapter 11
Chinese Tea and Alcohol
中国茶和酒

Major Topics
一、酒店知识：Chinese Drinking Practices 中国人的饮酒习惯
二、酒店员工：Beverage Manager 酒水部经理
　　　　　　　Bar Manager/Supervisor 酒吧经理/主管
　　　　　　　Head Bartender 酒吧领班
三、酒店视频：Chinese Drinking Etiquette 中国人的饮酒礼仪
四、酒店对话：Scenario 1: Recommending Chinese Alcohol 推荐中国酒
　　　　　　　Scenario 2: Taking Orders of Tea 为客人点茶
　　　　　　　Scenario 3: Recommending Chinese Tea 推荐中国茶
　　　　　　　Scenario 4: Chatting over Tea Ceremony 闲聊茶艺表演
五、巩固练习

　　This chapter deals with the topic of serving Chinese tea and alcohol. In *Part One*, you'll read ABC about Chinese drinking customs as a warming-up exercise. In *Part Two*, job description of working staff is provided for you to have some basics about the responsibility of each job at a Chinese restaurant. In *Part Three*, you'll watch a short video about Chinese drinking etiquette. In the next section, *Part Four* will provide some situational dialogues for you to practice the skills of serving Chinese tea and liquors based on different scenarios. *Part Five* includes additional exercises to enhance your understanding of Chinese tea or liquors, and get to know how to drink Chinese alcohol and tea in a right way.

Part One ABC for Hotel
一、酒店知识

Chinese Drinking Practices 中国人的饮酒习惯

Word Tips

internal /ɪnˈtɜːnəl/ *adj.* 内部的
strengthen /ˈstreŋθn/ *v.* 加强,巩固
constitution /ˌkɒnstɪˈtjuːʃən/ *n.* 结构,组织
soak /səʊk/ *v.* 浸泡;渗透
perpetuation /pəˌpetʃʊˈeɪʃn/ *n.* 永存,不朽
clink /klɪŋk/ *v.* 发出叮当声

sociality /ˌsəʊʃɪˈælɪtɪ/ *n.* 社会性,群居性
jeopardize /ˈdʒepədaɪz/ *v.* 危及,影响
sip /sɪp/ *v.* 呷,小口喝
highlight /ˈhaɪlaɪt/ *v.* 强调,使突出
intertwine /ˌɪntəˈtwaɪn/ *v.* 缠结,盘结
cling to 依附;贪恋

In China, alcohol has internal connection with sociality. Drinking provides more chances for one to make more friends as the old saying says, "Frequent drinking makes friends surrounding." Moreover, alcohol also serves effectively to deepen and strengthen friendship. Since it shows one's friendliness, alcohol is always used to relieve misunderstanding and hatred no matter how strong they are.

Chinese people believe that moderate drinking of alcohol is good for one's health and excessive drinking will jeopardize one's physical constitution. As a result, few Chinese, although there are some, will cling to bottles. However, many Chinese do sip a little alcohol at times to keep them fresh and healthy. Some even soak traditional Chinese medicine in liquor to achieve better effect, which has proven effective.

Most people drink alcohol just for entertainment. It is used to add to the fun of festive times, to highlight the happy and exciting moment. Sitting at tables and playing drinking games, with glasses clinking, people will soar up both physically and mentally with the aid of nature's most precious medicine: alcohol. Unfortunately, there are always some drunk people after too much consumption.

Drinking in China is not only about pleasure; it has much to do with respect, self-affirmation, friendship and the perpetuation of tradition. In China, no wedding ceremony is complete unless the bride and groom perform the traditional jiaobeijiu, which requires the couple to drink from each other's glasses while intertwining their arms, without spilling alcohol. The jiaobeijiu is followed by a dutiful toast to each of the newlyweds' parents.

The fact that drinking is so deeply rooted in Chinese culture worries doctors who specialize in alcohol abuse, and some are calling for changes in drinking practices. A law that forbids the sale of beverages with an alcohol content of 0.5 per cent or higher to anyone under age 18 has taken effect.

Based on the above passage, decide whether the following statements are true or false. Write T for true and F for false.

1. _____ Chinese take it for granted that drinking can relieve misunderstanding and hatred no matter how strong they are.
2. _____ Drinking of a little bit alcohol is good to one's health, but excessive drinking will do harm to one's physical constitution.
3. _____ Some Chinese soak traditional Chinese medicine in wine to enhance their health, which has proven effective.
4. _____ Sitting at tables and playing drinking games add to the fun of festive times, to highlight the happy and exciting moment.
5. _____ Drinking is deeply rooted in Chinese culture. Anyone who wants to change Chinese drinking practices is doomed to failure.

Part Two Working Staff
二、酒店员工

1 Listen to the job description of each one in the department, correct the mistakes and put the right ones in the blanks.

(1) **Beverage Manager** reports to Food and Beverage Manager, oversees the purchase and supply of beverages. Main obligations are:

To update the drink order.

To watch the beverage market, dealing with drinks supplies and pricing.

To maintain inventory and restock beverage.

To direct and supervise employees working with beverages.

To promote beverage sales.

   a. _____

   b. _____

中文提示：

    酒水部经理：向餐饮部经理汇报，监督饮料销售和供应。主要职责有更新饮料清单，掌握饮料市场动态，采购饮料并定价，管理饮料库存、进货，指导、监督员工工作，负责饮料促销。

(2) **Bar Manager/Supervisor** reports to Beverage Manager, taking charge of daily operations of bars.

To schedule staff.

To train employees.

To review the stored beverage and keep records of supplies and money.

To contact customers.

    a. _____
    b. _____

中文提示：

　　酒吧经理/主管：向酒水部经理汇报，主管酒吧日常工作，酒吧人员工作分配任务，培训员工，管理库存、现金，联络客户。

(3) **Head Bartender** reports to Bars Manager/Supervisor, takes charge of the overall bar area of his shift:

To order supplies and liquor.

To oversees other bartenders' performance.

To make and serve wines.

To communicate with guests, promote the sales of liquors and beverages.

    a. _____
    b. _____

中文提示：

　　酒吧领班：向酒吧经理/主任汇报，主管酒吧当班班次工作：领取酒品，安排、监督吧员工作，调酒、上酒，与客人交谈，负责酒品、饮料促销。

2 Listen again and discuss the job description of the post you wish to hold in your career.

Part Three　Video for the Hotel
三、酒店视频

Chinese Drinking Etiquette 中国人的饮酒礼仪

Word Tips

generalization /ˌdʒenrəlaɪˈzeɪʃn/ n. 通则，普遍化
toast /təʊst/ v. 祝酒，干杯
inferior /ɪnˈfɪəriə(r)/ adj. 次等的，下级的
rim /rɪm/ n. 边，边缘
depend on 取决于

throughout /θruːˈaʊt/ prep. 遍及，贯穿
humble /ˈhʌmbl/ adj. 谦逊的
drop /drɒp/ v. 降低
rambunctious /ræmˈbʌŋkʃəs/ adj. 喧闹的
take place 发生

A Watch the video twice, and decide whether the following statements are true or false according to the video.

1. _____ Drinking is a very important part of the Chinese dining etiquette.
2. _____ It isn't really something that the Chinese people look forward to, and they enjoy drinking together.
3. _____ Sometimes when toast goes on, people start to get drunk because they play drinking games.
4. _____ When you touch your glasses, it's important that you drop your hand a little bit, so the rim of your glass touches below.
5. _____ You cannot refuse to drink when people repeatedly ask you no matter you're Chinese or not.

B Watch the video again, and answer the following questions.

1. What do Americans normally do when they propose a toast at meals?
   _____.

2. Why does the speaker suggest you lower your glass a bit when your glass touch the glass of the person you toast?
   _____.

3. What is the general rule about whom to toast in a Chinese dinner situation?
   _____.

4. What is the speaker's attitude towards drinking games at a Chinese dinner?
   _____.

5. Does the speaker believe the statement that you cannot simply do business in China if you don't drink?
   _____.

Part Four Dialogues in the Hotel
四、酒店对话

Scenario 1

Recommending Chinese Alcohol 推荐中国酒

A Listen to Dialogue 1, and complete the following conversation with what you hear.

Waiter (W): Good evening! Would you like some wine? Here is the (1) _____.
Guest (G): Yes. What would you recommend?
W: Since you ordered Chinese food, I'd suggest you try some Chinese wine. We have Chinese rice wine and (2) _____.

G: Are there any differences between them?
W: Yes. Chinese rice wine is made from rice or (3) _____ , while the Chinese spirits is made from (4)_____, wheat or Chinese sorghum.
G: Which is stronger, the rice wine or the spirits?
W: The spirits are much stronger. People from southern China prefer (5) _____ while those from the north drink spirits.
G: I don't like strong liquor. Do you have something soft to drink?
W: If you prefer mild liquor, I think the Chinese yellow wine will be (6) _____ and it will go well with the crab you ordered.
G: Fine. We'd like some Shaoxing Jia Fan Jiu.

B Divide your class into groups of two or three students, and do the dialogue again.

Scenario 2

Taking Orders of Tea 为客人点茶

A Listen to Dialogue 2 and write numbers in the blanks to show the correct order of the conversation.

_____ **Waiter (W):** What kind of tea would you like to try?
_____ W: I'll be back with your tea shortly.
_____ **Guest (G):** I think we'd like to try the Oolong tea.
_____ G: Yes, that's good. What kind of fruit do you serve right now?
_____ G: Two tea cups, please.
_____ W: Have you had enough time to look at the menu?
_____ G: That sounds nice. I'd like one.
_____ W: Do you want a cup or a pot of tea?
_____ W: Today, the fresh fruit platter includes watermelon, strawberries, apples and oranges.
_____ G: Yes, I think we're ready to order.
_____ W: Would you like some snacks?
_____ G: A pot of tea, please.
_____ W: How many tea cups would you like?

B Role play: One student plays the role of waiter while another plays the role of guest.

Scenario 3

Recommending Chinese Tea 推荐中国茶

A Listen to Dialogue 3 and fill in the table with relevant information.

Gender of the guest	Green tea	Black tea	Jasmine tea	Tea ordered

B Listen to the dialogue again, and do a situational dialogue with your partner.

Waiter (W): What can I do for you, madam?

Guest (G): I'd like some tea, please.

W: What tea do you prefer?

G: Green tea, please.

W: We have got Longjing Tea, which is from Hangzhou and Bi Luo Chun from Jiangsu.

G: I've heard a lot about Longjing Tea. So, Longjing Tea, please. By the way, is there any other tea in China?

W: Of course, there is. The most famous is Oolong. It's said that it can help people reduce weight.

G: Really? You mean I should drink some Oolong, don't you?

W: No. I should say you're slim and green tea is the wisest choice, especially in summer.

G: Thank you. What's jasmine tea?

W: Oh, it's a kind of green tea with the smell of jasmine. Beijing people like it very much. They prefer a strong tasting tea.

G: I see.

W: Would you like your tea now, madam?

G: Yes, please.

W: A cup of Longjing Tea for you.

G: Yes.

Scenario 4

Chatting over Tea Ceremony 闲聊茶艺表演

A Listen to Dialogue 4 and mark the following sentences with T(true) or F(false).
1. _____ The guests are new to China and they've never watched a tea ceremony before.
2. _____ The tea house provides tea ceremonies performances for those regular guests.
3. _____ They have to pay for ceremony, but the tea and snacks are complimentary.
4. _____ The actress from a troupe will have a tea performance to please the guests.

B Listen to the dialogue again and answer the following questions.
1. Where do the guests drink tea?
   _____.
2. Does the tea house offer any shows about tea art and tea techniques?
   _____.
3. Who will present the tea performance?
   _____.
4. What programs does the tea ceremony have?
   _____.

Waiter (W): Welcome to the Old City Tea House. How may I help you?
Guest (G): Do you have tea ceremony performances?
W: Yes, would you like to watch one?
G: Yes, we're new to China and we've never been to a tea ceremony before.
W: We can have one of our waitresses come out and give you a private performance.
G: May I ask how much it costs?
W: The ceremony is free, but you have to pay for the tea and snacks.
G: OK, that sounds very reasonable. What does the tea ceremony include?
W: You will find out how to pour tea correctly, what kind of tea pots you should use with certain types of tea leaves, and even how to read tea leaves.
G: That's great. When can we start?
W: I'll bring the waitresses over and start the ceremony now.

Additional Exercises:

Divide the class into groups. Each group makes a situational dialogue using words and phrase for Chinese tea and alcohol. You may refer to the working procedures or sentence patterns in Dialogue 1, Dialogue 2, Dialogue 3 and Dialogue 4.

Additional Words and Phrases 更多的词汇短语储备

Word Tips

一、酒类

黄酒类 Yellow Wine
陈年彩坛花雕 Caitan Huadiao Medium Sweet
女儿红12年 Nu'er Hong (12 Years)
青瓷五年 Qingci Huadiao (5 Years) Medium Sweet

白酒类 Liquor
红星二锅头52度 Red Star Erguotou (500ml 52°)
金六福(五星)52度 Jinliufu (Five-Star) (52°)
国窖1573 Guo Jiao 1573 (The First Cellar in China)

啤酒 Beer
百威啤酒 Budweiser　　　　　　嘉士伯啤酒 Carlsberg
青岛扎啤 Tsing Tao Draught

二、茶类

1、绿茶 Green Tea
Maojian Tea (Green Tea)毛尖茶　　　　Xinyang Maojian Tea (Green Tea)信阳毛尖
Junshan Silver Needle Tea 君山银针　　Yellow Mountain Fuzz Tip 黄山毛峰

2、红茶 Black Tea
Keemun Black Tea 祁门红茶　　　　　Earl Grey Tea 伯爵茶
Assorted Chinese Herbal Tea 八宝茶　　Greengage Black Tea 梅子红茶

3、花茶 Scented Tea
Jasmine Tea 茉莉花茶　　　　　　　Chrysanthemum Tea 菊花茶
Jasmine Silver Needle Tea 茉莉大白毫　Peony Jasmine Tea 牡丹绣球

4、茶饮料 Tea Drinks
Iced Black Tea / Iced Green Tea 冰红(绿)茶　Iced Milk Tea 冰奶茶
Hot Tea, HK Style 港式奶茶　　　　　　　Chocolate Milk Tea 巧克力奶茶
Iced Chocolate Milk Tea 冰巧克力奶茶

Part Five   Consolidation
五、巩固练习

A Fill the blanks with the basic knowledge about Chinese tea and alcohol you've learnt.

1. People drink _____ to show respect to the Chinese patriotic poet Qu Yuan.
2. _____ is regarded as the national liquor in China.
3. White wine is kind of grape wine rather than _____.
4. Tea compressed into the shape of brick is called _____.
5. _____ has been fermented, then heated to give its characteristic deep, dark colors.
6. Dried flowers are added to a variety of green tea, which turns out to be _____.

B Translation

i. Translate the following sentences into Chinese.
  1. Drinking provides more chances for one to make more friends as the old saying says(古言道), "Frequent drinking makes friends surrounding."
  2. Chinese people believe that moderate drinking of alcohol is good for one's health and excessive drinking will jeopardize(危害) one's physical constitution.
  3. Alcohol in China may be used to add to the fun of festive times(节庆时), to highlight the happy and exciting moment.
  4. People from southern China prefer rice wine(米酒) while those from the north drink spirits.
  5. So, in a sense, wine or spirit is both lubricant(润滑剂) and adhesive(黏合剂) of Chinese culture.

ii. Translate the following sentences into English.
  1. 一日三餐一茶对于中国人来说是生活之必需(daily necessity)。
  2. 中国最有名的红茶(black tea)是乌龙茶,可以帮助人们减肥。
  3. 我们餐厅有乌龙茶、红茶、绿茶、茉莉花茶以及菊花茶(Chrysanthemum tea)。你要什么呢?
  4. 我喜欢手工酿造的啤酒(craft beer)。再给我另一杯(make it two)。
  5. 他是一个酒鬼(heavy drinker),可以喝一打啤酒。他还清醒着(stone sober)呢。

C Writing

Advertisement 广告

No matter how great your hotel is, no one will ever know unless you advertise it. Write concisely, yet truthfully. Make sure to use selling adjectives such as "best," "great," "excellent," and "effective." Think about the possibility of offering a first time incentive. A free sample, trial or even a money-back guarantee will draw customers to your product. You may invite guests to taste one new tea, or you may allow them to enjoy the new liquor with 50% discount. In order to spark the interest of your regular guests, you may also offer them a few free bottles of wines.

Suppose you're the manager of Food & Beverage Department in the hotel, write an advertisement to promote the beverage in your bar.

Outline:
1. Name of the wine, liquor or tea
2. The features of each wine or tea
3. Location of the bar
4. Service hours
5. How to make reservations (Tel. No.)

Chapter 12
Room Service
送餐服务

Major Topics 一、酒店知识：How Does Room Service Work? 怎样做好客房用餐服务?
二、酒店员工：Room Service Supervisor 送餐服务主管
Room Service Attendant 送餐服务员
三、酒店视频：Crowne Plaza Smartware In-room Dining Service 皇冠假日酒店送餐服务
四、酒店对话：Scenario 1: Calling for Breakfast in Room 早餐送餐电话预订
Scenario 2: Room Service for Dinner 正餐送餐服务
Scenario 3: Delivering Food Orders to Guest Rooms 客房送餐
Scenario 4: Handling Complaints about Room Service 处理送餐服务投诉
五、巩固练习

This chapter concentrates on the topic of room service in a hotel. In *Part One*, you'll read ABC about room service and understand how it will be handled as a warming-up exercise. In *Part Two*, job description of working staff is provided for you to have some basics about the responsibility of each job in the department. In *Part Three*, you'll watch a short video about a new trend of in-room dining service in a hotel. In the next section, *Part Four* will provide some situational dialogues for you to practice room service based on different scenarios. *Part Five* includes additional exercises to enhance your knowledge and skills about in-room dining service, and get to know how to call for room service in an appropriate way.

Part One ABC for Hotel
一、酒店知识

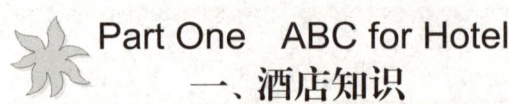
How Does Room Service Work? 怎样做好客房用餐服务？

Word Tips

significant /sɪgˈnɪfɪkənt/ adj. 重要的；有意义的
cabin /ˈkæbɪn/ n. 小木屋；客舱
specification /ˌspesɪfɪˈkeɪʃn/ n. 规格；详述
cart /kɑːt/ n. 手推车
itemize /ˈaɪtəmaɪz/ v. 列出清单
accouterment /əˈkuːtəmənts/ n. 装饰；配备

originate /əˈrɪdʒɪneɪt/ v. 引起；创始
hallway /ˈhɔːlweɪ/ n. 走廊；门厅
lid /lɪd/ n. 盖子
dismiss /dɪsˈmɪs/ v. 让……离开；解散
gratuity /grəˈtjuːəti/ n. 报酬；小费

Room service works in similar ways to regular restaurant service. The customer places an order, the cooks make the food, and the server delivers it. It does, however, have its significant differences. For one, room service originates from your hotel room, cabin, or other guest lodging. Secondly, the servers don't generally check in on you repeatedly throughout the course of your meal. Lastly, you simply have to take your dishes out into the hallway, leaving it for hotel staff.

Some hotels provide guests with room service menus, and higher-end hotels serve chef's specials and guest requests. The guest calls room service directly, or calls the front desk or concierge to be connected to room service. Some guests call the concierge for recommendations on what to order and what the house specialties are. Then a room service attendant, a desk attendant or other hotel staff member takes the meal order via phone.

These orders are delivered to the kitchen staff and the meal is prepared as per the guest's specifications. The meals are then topped with lids or other covers and placed on special room service carts or trays to be delivered. The room service attendant prepares the cart, making sure the guest has everything she may need, and delivers the cart to the hotel room.

When the waiter arrives with the meal, the guest may dismiss him, or ask him to set up and serve the meal. The room service waiter will present the guest with an itemized bill for the order. Some establishments include a gratuity on the bill, while others leave the choice for gratuity up to the guest. If the bill has a gratuity included, it is not necessary to tip the waiter again, unless the guest feels he would like to. If the bill does not include a gratuity charge, it is customary service etiquette to reward the server for a job well done. Standard tip amounts are 15% to 20%. Guests usually do not have to pay their room service bill when their meal arrives. They can elect to charge it to their room and pay all fees at checkout.

After the meal is finished, and depending on the hotel, guests can either clean up their own meals, or call for a hotel staff member to do so. Guests who elect to clean up themselves can place their dishes and dinner accouterments on the delivery cart and place it in the hallway outside the door or in an out-of-the-way spot in the room. In some hotels, guests can call the room service attendant back to the room to clear the meal and remove the dishes. Other guests elect to leave the meal as it is and allow housekeeping to attend to it.

Based on the above passage, decide whether the following statements are true or false. Write T for true and F for false.

1. _____ The way room service works is the same as that of regular restaurant service.
2. _____ A guest has to call the room service department if he/she wants to request in-room meal service.
3. _____ For room service, the guest does not need to tip the room service attendant as gratuity is always included in the bill.
4. _____ Hotels usually offer options for guests to choose as to how they would like the dishes to be cleared after they have finished the meal.

Part Two   Working Staff
二、酒店员工

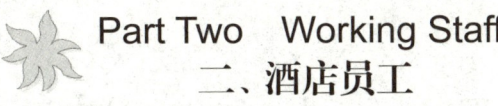

1 Listen to the job description of each one in the department, correct the mistakes and put the right ones in the blanks.

(1) **Room Service Supervisor**

Room Service Supervisor reports to Food and Beverage Manager. His basic responsibilities are to plan, organize, control and direct the work of employees in the room service while ensuring guest satisfaction.

To work closely with the manager of the kitchen.

To coordinate and oversee all room service operations.

To assign duties and responsibilities to employees in accordance with work procedures.

To purchase supplies and equipment needed to ensure quality and timely delivery of services.

a. _____

b. _____

中文提示：

送餐服务主管： 向餐饮部经理汇报，主要职责是计划、组织、监管和指导客房送餐员工的工作，为客人提供满意的服务；密切配合厨房经理的工作，协调和监督送餐服务，根据送餐工作程序给员工分配下达任务，订购设备、提供补给，确保送餐服务时效和质量。

(2) **Room Service Attendant**

Room Service Waiter/Waitress reports straight to Room Service Supervisor:
To take orders from guests for food or beverages.
To stock service areas with supplies such as coffee, food, tableware, and napkins.
To get ready tableware, trays, etc. for food delivery.
To send food orders to guest's rooms.
To obtain signatures on the bill or collect cash.
To take away tableware and clean the room after guests finish dining.

a. _____
b. _____

中文提示：

送餐服务员：向送餐服务主管汇报；接受客人订餐，做好配餐工作，如准备咖啡、食物、餐具、餐巾等；准备好送餐车、托盘等；送餐至客人房间；请客人签单或付款；客人用餐后清理餐具，打扫卫生。

2 Listen again and discuss the job description of the post you wish to hold in your career.

Part Three　Video for the Hotel
三、酒店视频

Crowne Plaza In-room Dining Service 皇冠假日酒店送餐服务

Word Tips

client /ˈklaɪənt/ n. 主顾
vase /vɑːz/ n. 装饰瓶，花瓶
strawberry /ˈstrɔːbəri/ n. 草莓；草莓色
laptop /ˈlæptɒp/ n. 便携式电脑
metaphor /ˈmetəfə(r)/ n. 隐喻，暗喻
soggy /ˈsɒɡi/ adj. 湿透的，浸透的
grail /ɡreɪl/ n. 杯；盘
flexible /ˈfleksəbl/ adj. 灵活的；柔韧的

emulate /ˈemjuleɪt/ v. 模仿；努力赶上
category /ˈkætəɡəri/ n. 类型；部门
cookies n. 甜饼干
greasy /ˈɡriːsi/ adj. 油腻的；谄媚的
multitude /ˈmʌltɪtjuːd/ adj. 大量，许多
holy /ˈhəʊli/ adj. 神圣的；值得尊敬的
crack /kræk/ v. 破裂

A Watch the video twice, and decide whether the following statements are true or false according to the video.

1. _____ According to the speaker, room service in the past was good because the hotel tried to create a setting of restaurant in guests' rooms.
2. _____ Creation of in-room dining menu should be based on what people are doing in their rooms at the hotel.
3. _____ According to the speaker, when delivering the food, the hotel staff should bring some small gifts to the guest along with the food.
4. _____ The big problem in sending up food from the kitchen to the guest's room is keeping food hot without making food uncomfortably wet.

B Watch the video again, and answer the following questions.

1. How did clients update their guest experience?
   _____.

2. Why does the speaker say "it just has a reputation for being done poorly"?
   _____.

3. When we create a new menu for people, it is categorized not based on lunch, dinner, and breakfast. What is it based on?
   _____.

4. Besides what the speaker referred to, what else did we need to consider when creating a total system that really addressed the multitude of food options?
   _____.

5. What's the big problem we face when delivering food to guest rooms?
   _____.

Part Four Dialogues in the Hotel
四、酒店对话

Scenario 1

Calling for Breakfast in Room 早餐送餐电话预订

A Listen to Dialogue 1, and complete the following conversation with what you hear.

Receptionist (R): Yes, madam. May I help you?
Ann (A): Hello, this is Ann in (1)_____. Can I order some room service?
R: Yes, you can. What would you like?
A: I'd like to have breakfast in room. What time do you (2)_____ in the morning?

R: We usually start from seven. But if you have special needs you can tell (3)_____ the night before.
A: Oh, but...
R: Or you can also tell me now. We'll send your food over at your (4)_____.
A: Very good, Could you send two (5)_____ to our room at 6:30 tomorrow morning? We must leave the hotel before 7:00.
R: No problem. So Room 1215, two American breakfasts, (6)_____ tomorrow morning.
A: That's right.

B Divide your class into groups of two or three students, and do the dialogue again.

Scenario 2

Room Service for Dinner 正餐送餐服务

A Listen to Dialogue 2 and write numbers in the blanks to show the correct order of the conversation.

_____ **Guest (G):** Room Service, please.
_____ **Receptionist (R):** Yes, sir. May I help you?
_____ G: Got it, thanks.
_____ R: Good. We'll be up in a couple of minutes.
_____ R: Yes, sir. What would you like?
_____ R: May I have your name and your room number?
_____ G: I'll take the tuna, and how long will it take?
_____ G: I'll have a sandwich and a hot chocolate.
_____ R: It should be ready in a few minutes.
_____ G: Can I still get something to eat at this time of night?
_____ R: What kind of sandwich would you like? We have steak, cheese, ham, salami, tuna, chicken.
_____ G: Bob Jackson, Room 801.

B Role play: One student plays the role of receptionist while another plays the role of guest.

Scenario 3

Delivering Food Orders to Guest Rooms 客房送餐

A Listen to Dialogue 3 and fill in the table with correct information.

Item	Orange juice	Sandwiches	Coffee	Service charge
Price				
Total				

B Listen to the dialogue again, and do a situational dialogue with your partner.

Waitress(W): Room service. May I come in?

Jason(J): Come in, please.

W: Mr. Jason, I've brought you your breakfast ordered. Where shall I put it?

J: Oh, yes, thank you. Just put them on the desk over there.

W: All right. Here are your orange juice, tuna sandwiches, your mustard, ketchup and your coffee. Shall I pour a cup of coffee straight away, sir?

J: No, thanks. I'll pour it in a minute myself.

W: One more thing, sir. The orange juice is 15 *Yuan*, the sandwiches are 25 *Yuan* each and the coffee is 20 *Yuan*. That comes 60 *Yuan*, plus 15% service charge. The total is 69 *Yuan*, and here is your bill.

J: Thank you. Can I have it charged to my account, please?

W: Certainly, sir. Please sign your name and room number here on the bill. Thank you for using room service. If you need anything else, please dial "7" or press the button over there. Please enjoy your breakfast and have a nice day. Goodbye.

J: Goodbye.

Scenario 4

Handling Complaints about Room Service 处理送餐服务投诉

A Listen to Dialogue 4 and decide whether the statements are True or False.

_____ The breakfast that the guest ordered was quickly served.

_____ The guest made his order by note.

_____ It was the housekeeper's mistake to leave out the order.

_____ The restaurant and the cafeteria on the ground floor are closed.

_____ The chef did apologize to the guest for his carelessness.

B Listen to the dialogue again and answer the following questions.

1. What did the guest complain about?
   _____

2. When did the guest make his order?
   _____

3. Why did the chef neglect the guest's order?
   _____

4. Did the guest forgive the mistake or forget it?
   _____

Waiter (W): Hello. Room Service. What's the matter?

Guest (G): I ordered breakfast last night. Now it is already fifteen past eight and my order hasn't been served yet!

W: Sorry, sir. How did you make your order?

G: By phone.

W: Please hold on and I'll check it for you right away... I'm really regretful for it, sir. It is our mistake. We're putting your order in a wrong place, so the chef had no knowledge about it.

G: It's terrible.

W: The restaurant and the cafeteria on the ground floor are serving now and you can go there.

G: Well, I'll go downstairs.

W: We are sorry that we didn't provide you a better service.

G: Forget it.

Additional Exercises:

Divide the class into groups. Each group makes a situational dialogue using words or phrases for the Room Service. You may refer to the working procedures or sentence patterns in Dialogue 1, Dialogue 2, Dialogue 3 and Dialogue 4.

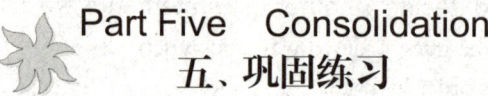

Part Five   Consolidation
五、巩固练习

A Match column A with column B, and make a dialogue with your partner.

1. Room service, may I come in?   A. Yes, sir. May I help you?
2. Shall I place it here?   B. Come in, please.

3. May I have your name and room number?
4. Is that Room Service?
5. How long will it take?

C. It should be ready in about 10 minutes.
D. Yes, on the table is fine.
E. This is Bob Jackson, Room 302.

B Translation

i. Translate the following sentences into Chinese.

1. If you want breakfast in your room tomorrow morning, call Room Service tonight and place your order (点餐).
2. I'd like to have two hot roast-beef sandwiches and a large pot (壶) of coffee sent up to my room right now.
3. Please tell me your room number and the time you want us to wake you up (叫醒).
4. Okay. I'll bring an ice bucket (一桶冰块) along with some water for you. Is there anything else you need me to bring up to your room?
5. Room Service. What kind of sandwich would you like? We have steak, cheese, ham, salami (意大利香肠), tuna (金枪鱼) and chicken.

ii. Translate the following sentences into English.

1. 如果您想喝点什么,您可以叫送餐服务或自己下来,酒吧就在大厅(lobby)的后面。
2. 酒店将继续提供传统的送餐服务,这些新品和饮料会迎合(cater to)当今旅游者不断变化的需求。
3 你们明天早上6点半能不能送(send)两份美式早餐过来？我们7点前必须离开酒店。
4. 或者您现在告诉我也可以,我们会按您要求(requested)的时间送餐的。
5 这是您的挂门餐牌(door menu)。检查一下您早餐要吃什么,标上时间,今天晚上睡觉之前,挂在门上。

C Writing

Door Knob Menu 门把式菜单

Room service attendants deliver food, drinks, silverware and condiments to guest rooms to fulfill guest orders. They wheel the tray into the guest room, sets up the table, opens platters and identifies each portion. The attendant may check back later to remove the cart.

Suppose you want to have your breakfast delivered in your room, mark the items and time on the door knob menu and hang it outside the door. The room attendant will deliver the order of food as you request.

Outline:
1. Room Number
2. Dishes requested
3. Delivery time
4. Other services if necessary

Chapter 13

Banquet Service
宴会服务

Major Topics
一、酒店知识：Types of Banquet Service 宴会服务类型
二、酒店员工：Conference and Banqueting Manager 会议宴会经理
　　　　　　　Conference and Banqueting Sales Manager 会议宴会销售经理
　　　　　　　Banqueting Headwaiter 宴会服务人员主管
　　　　　　　Banqueting Waiter and Wine Waiter 宴会服务员和斟酒服务员
三、酒店视频：How to Decorate Tables for Weddings? 如何装饰婚宴餐桌？
四、酒店对话：Scenario 1: Inquiries about the Banquet 宴会咨询
　　　　　　　Scenario 2. Meeting Service 会议服务
　　　　　　　Scenario 3. Banquet Menu 宴会菜单
　　　　　　　Scenario 4. A Banquet 举办晚宴
五、巩固练习

　　This chapter concentrates on the banquet service in a hotel. In *Part One*, you'll read ABC about types of banquet service as a warming-up exercise. In *Part Two*, job description of working staff is provided for you to have some basics about the responsibility of each job in the Banqueting and Conference Department. In *Part Three*, you'll watch a short video about the table decoration of a wedding party. In the next section, *Part Four* will provide some situational dialogues for you to practice the banquet services based on different scenarios. *Part Five* includes additional exercises to enhance your knowledge and skills of banquet service.

Part One ABC for Hotel
一、酒店知识

Types of Banquet Service 宴会服务类型

Word Tips

event /ɪˈvent/ n. 节事，节庆
attendee /ˌætenˈdiː/ n. 出席者
buffet /ˈbʊfeɪ/ n. 自助餐
replenish /rɪˈplenɪʃ/ v. 补充
circulate /ˈsɜːkjəleɪt/ v. 循环；(使)流通

entree /ˈɒntreɪ/ n. 主菜
elegant /ˈelɪɡənt/ adj. 优美的；漂亮的
picky /ˈpɪkɪ/ adj. 好挑剔的，过分讲究的
mingle /ˈmɪŋɡl/ v. 混合，混淆
scheduled /ˈʃedjuːld/ adj. 预订的，按计划的

Planning a banquet requires you to make decisions concerning the arrangements for the event. In addition to deciding what foods and beverages the attendees of your banquet will eat and drink, you must also decide how they will receive that food. Each type of banquet service has its own benefits and considerations.

Sit-down Service

With sit-down service, your banquet guests receive their food at their seats. Typically, you offer a choice of entrees, such as a beef, chicken, fish or vegetarian dinner and have attendees make selections ahead of time.

This requires extra work in the planning stages of the event as you will need to keep track of not only who is attending, but who has made dinner selections and what those dinner selections were. Banquet hosts often opt for sit-down service despite the added planning because it is generally considered the most elegant of service types. Sit-down service is generally the most expensive type of banquet dining.

Buffet Service

A long line of hot and cold foods placed along one or more tables is the main characteristic of buffet service. Guests form one or two lines and walk alongside the buffet table, choosing what food they wish to eat.

Buffet service is generally regarded as less elegant than seated service since guests are required to at least go and get their meals on their own. The cost is typically lower for a buffet meal, however, and it often allows for a greater number of meal choices for picky attendees.

Station Service

Station service is a modified form of buffet service, and typically costs somewhere between the price of a buffet and a sit-down meal. At a station service banquet, small tables are set up around the banquet room. Each station features a different kind of food and is typically staffed by a banquet server who keeps the food replenished and, in some cases, prepares or serves it.

Station service encourages guests to move about the room and mingle with other attendees, while still having tables available for guests to return to and enjoy their meals during a scheduled dinner hour. Because stations are less common than other types of banquets, they often maintain a more elegant feel than a traditional buffet.

Passed-tray Service

With passed-tray service, the wait staff circulates through the banquet room with finger foods on large platters. The servers approach guests and offer food and a napkin. The service typically operates continuously for a block of time, and a full meal may not be served.

Passed-tray service encourages conversation and is typically considered more elegant than a buffet. The cost of a passed-tray event varies based upon the types of foods you select and how long you wish for the service to continue and may or may not be more expensive than a buffet.

Based on the above passage, decide whether the following statements are true or false. Write T for true and F for false.

1. _____ Many banquet hosts would not like to choose sit-down service because it involves too much extra planning work.
2. _____ One advantage of buffet service over seated service is that the former can allow the guests to have the food they like.
3. _____ Station service is similar to buffet service but appears more elegant than the latter.
4. _____ As passed-tray service requires more waiting staff, it costs much more than buffet service.
5. _____ According to the passage, a wedding banquet host should choose sit-down service because it is the most expensive and elegant of all service types.

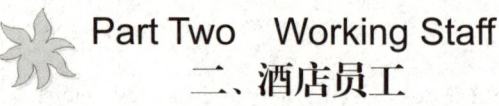

Part Two   Working Staff
二、酒店员工

1 Listen to the job description of each one in the department, correct the mistakes and put the right ones in the blanks.

(1) **Conference and Banqueting Manager** reports to Food & Beverage Manager, oversees all aspects of a banquet or event. His responsibilities are:

To supervise the operations of the Conferencing and Banqueting Department.

To keep in touch with the sales department.

To plan and coordinate the details of a banquet, including creating wine list and restocking supplies requested.

To keep in touch with the customer during the activities.

To coordinate with the staff.

a. _____

b. _____

中文提示：

　　会议宴会经理：向餐饮部经理汇报，管理宴会或节庆活动各个方面的事务，监督宴会会议部的运作和管理；与销售部联系，组织和协调宴会的具体安排事项，包括制定菜单和采购宴会用品；负责与客户在活动期间的联络，协调员工之间的工作。

(2) **Conference and Banqueting Sales Manager** is the head of the Conferencing and Banqueting Department, who reports to Conference and Banqueting Manager.

To make sales budget for banquet events, including time for events, menus, pricing, employee schedules, etc.

To coordinate the planning and execution of meetings, banquets and food outlets.

To communicate with customers before, during and after event.

a. _____

b. _____

中文提示：

　　会议宴会销售经理：负责会议宴会部的全面工作，向会议宴会经理汇报；其主要职责是制订销售计划，包括活动日期、菜单、价格、员工配备等；协调会议、宴会和餐饮的组织、筹备和实施工作；负责与客户活动前后以及过程中的联络工作。

(3) **Banqueting Headwaiter** reports to Conference and Banqueting Manager, and coordinates the work of all employees in a function room.

a. _____

b. _____

中文提示：

　　宴会服务人员主管：向会议宴会经理汇报，负责协调功能厅所有服务人员的工作。

(4) **Banqueting Waiter and Wine Waiter** perform duties that are similar to those of the wait staff in a restaurant:

To take food and drink orders for guests.

To deliver orders to the bar and kitchen.

To deliver the foods and drinks to the customer's table.

To process cash and credit bill payment transactions.

To do other duties, such as cleaning the tables, adding ingredient bottles, etc.

a. _____
b. _____

中文提示：

  宴会服务员和斟酒服务员：履行与餐厅服务员相同的职责；为客人点餐；传菜单到酒吧和厨房；上菜、酒水至顾客餐桌；现金、支票结账；清洁桌面或添加调味品等。

2 Listen again and discuss the job description of the post you wish to hold in your career.

Part Three   Video for the Hotel
三、酒店视频

How to Decorate Tables for Weddings 如何装饰婚宴餐桌

Word Tips

decorate /ˈdekəreɪt/ v. 装饰；点缀
china /ˈtʃaɪnə/ n. 瓷器；瓷餐具
flatware /ˈflætweə(r)/ n. 扁平的餐具
approximate /əˈprɒksɪmət/ adj. 大概的；极相似的
extra /ˈekstrə/ adj. 额外的，补充的
centerpiece /ˈsentəpiːs/ n. 中心装饰品

drape /dreɪp/ v. 悬挂，成褶皱状垂下
stemware /ˈstemweə(r)/ n. 高脚杯；高脚器皿
napkin /ˈnæpkɪn/ n. 餐巾，餐巾纸
edge /edʒ/ n. 边缘，端
spectacular /spekˈtækjʊlə(r)/ adj. 富丽的，壮观的
glorious /ˈɡlɔːrɪəs/ adj. 辉煌的；荣誉的

A Watch the video twice, and fill in the blanks according to the video.

Step One: Set china about (1) _____ from the edge of the table.
Step Two: Place (2) _____ under the plate to add some drama.
Step Three: Set (3) _____ in the way people can use them from the outside in.
Step Four: Then add (4) _____ .
Step Five: Put a beautiful napkin and napkin ring (5) _____ the plate.
Step Six: Place (6) _____ in the middle of the table.

B Watch the video again, and answer the following questions.

1. What will you need when you decorate a table for a perfectly beautiful wedding table?
   _____.

2. To start with decoration of the table, where will you put the china on the table?
   _____.

3. Which do you think you should put first, the glassware or the flatware?
   _____.

4. On which side of the plate will you put the forks on the table, the left or the right?
   _____.

5. If you don't want to forget the center of attention for a perfect wedding table, what will you put on the table?
   _____.

Part Four Dialogues in the Hotel
四、酒店对话

Scenario 1

Inquiries about the Banquet 宴会咨询

A Listen to Dialogue 1, and fill out the table with the information you hear.

Time of the banquet	Date of the banquet	Number of attendees	Number of table	Items of Entertainment	Contact number

B Divide your class into groups of two or three students, and do the dialogue again.

Receptionist(R): Hello. How can I help you?

Jason(J): Hello, I'm Jason Deep. I'd like to organize a company banquet.

R: What date are you looking for?

J: The 20th of December.

R: What time do you want to start?

J: 6:00 p.m.

139

R: How many guests are you planning for?
J: There will be about 75 guests.
R: So, how do 8 tables sound?
J: That would be fine.
R: Have you thought about having any entertainment?
J: Does your hotel provide any?
R: We have singers and dancers who often perform at banquets.
J: Would it be possible to see a sample performance before we book them?
R: Certainly. We have a sample performance on our website that you can view.
J: Great. And could you give me details of costs?
R: Sure, sir. I'll forward a proposal to you before the end of the day. Can you give me your email?
J: It's ernestzhu@126.com. And our phone number is 84648219.
R: Thank you, sir. I'll be in touch very soon.
J: Thank you. Goodbye.

Scenario 2

Meeting Service 会议服务

A Listen to Dialogue 2 and write numbers in the blanks to show the correct order of the conversation.

_____ **Receptionist (R):** Good morning, Banqueting and Conferences. Can I help you?

_____ **Jack (J):** Yes. I'd like to ask some questions about the services your hotel can provide.

_____ R: Yes, the food is of very good quality.

_____ R: We can decorate the banquet hall in your company colors.

_____ J: We would like to have karaoke, can that be arranged?

_____ J: That's a good idea. Thank you.

_____ R: We also provide a band to play music and a toastmaster to lead the toast and introduce the speeches.

_____ R: Certainly, sir. We provide all the food. We can prepare a feast for you and your clients.

_____ J: What else do you provide?

_____ J: Is the food good quality?

_____ J: Good.

_____ R: Yes, we can also arrange to film the event and provide you with a DVD to watch.

B Role play: One student plays the role of receptionist while another plays the role of Jack.

Scenario 3

Banquet Menu 宴会菜单

A Listen to Dialogue 3 and complete the following dialogue.

Jason (J): What are the drinks for the banquet today?
Manager (M): Royal Salute, Dubonnet, sparkling cider and Martinis. And also very good rum punch.
J: Yes, it's very good. But we'd like to have (1) _____.
M: No problem. We'll use different colors and accessories that keep (2) _____ to your banquet.
J: That'll be fine. What about your waiters? Are they good?
M: And look at the waiters, please. They all look (3) _____. They're all wearing tuxedo jackets and a bow tie.
J: Yes, I've noticed that. What is on the menu for (4) _____?
M: There are snails in garlic butter, guinea hen under glass with wild rice, braised endive, heart of palm salad, and croquette.
J: Yes, French cuisine sounds marvelous. And please have (5) _____.
M: Certainly. And what would you like to (6) _____?
J: Vichyssoise. Please.
M: Yes. Wish you a happy night.

B Listen to the dialogue again, and do a situational dialogue with your partner.

Scenario 4

A Banquet 举办晚宴

A Decide whether the following statements are true (T) or false (F) according to the passage.

_____ 1. The guest ordered a dinner banquet for 15 people.
_____ 2. The banquet will start with Assorted Cold Dishes.
_____ 3. The guest is worried about her foreign friends. They may dislike the pigeon dish.
_____ 4. There are three kinds of dim sum for desserts.
_____ 5. A Fresh Fruit Platter and cups of Jasmine Tea will be served to conclude the dinner.

B Listen to the dialogue again and answer the following questions.

1. For how many people has the banquet been ordered?
   _____

2. Has the Banquet Manager got the menu ready?
   _____

3. What will the banquet start with?
   _____

4. How many kinds of dim sum will be served for desserts?
   _____

5. Will there be any fruit supplied for the banquet?
   _____

Banquet Manager (M): Good morning, Mrs. Beck. Glad to see you again.
Mrs. Beck (B): Glad to see you too. Last week we ordered a dinner banquet for 50 people. I'd like to discuss some of the details with you. Have you got the menu ready?
M: Certainly, madam. Here it is. The banquet will start with Assorted Cold Dishes. It's a collection of seafood, poultry and vegetable dishes. This is followed by the Shark's Fin Soup, then by Diced Chicken with Greed Pepper, Prawn in Tomato Sauce, Crispy Skinned Duck and Steamed Pigeon.
B: Wait a minute. I'm afraid my foreign friends won't like the pigeon dish. Can you change it for something else?
M: Sure. How about the Steamed Crab instead? Is that all right?
B: Yes. That sounds better.
M: There are two kinds of dim sum for desserts.
B: Can you tell me what they are?
M: Red Bean Cakes and Pumpkin Cakes.
B: That's all right. Is there any fruit and what about beverages?
M: Yes, Mrs. Beck. We'll serve a Fresh Fruit Platter and cups of Jasmine Tea to conclude the dinner.
B: Very good. Here is the deposit.
M: Thank you, Mrs. Beck.

Additional Words and Phrases 更多的词汇短语储备

Word Tips

1. 中餐餐具
tea set 茶具   plate 盘子   dish 碟子
saucer 茶碟   soup bowl 汤碗   cruet stand 调味品架

cruet 酱油醋瓶
mustard pot 芥末罐
sugar basin 糖罐

dessert plate 点心盘
table knife 餐刀
sugar tong 方糖夹

finger bowl 洗手盅
bread basket 面包蓝
milk jug 奶罐

2. 西餐餐具

dinner knife 主菜刀
lobster tong 龙虾钳
cake fork 蛋糕叉
sugar tong 糖夹
main course plate 主菜盆
butter dish 黄油碟
pitcher 冰水壶
champagne glass 香槟杯

dinner fork 主菜叉
fish knife 鱼刀
steak knife 牛排刀
ice tong 冰夹
soup plate 汤盆
coffee spoon 咖啡勺
wine basket 葡萄酒篮
starter plate 开胃品盘

snail tong 蜗牛夹
fish fork 鱼叉
carving knife 切肉刀
bottle opener 开瓶器
bread plate 面包盘
silver ware 银餐具
ice water glass 冰水杯
dessert plate 甜点盘

Part Five　Consolidation
五、巩固练习

A Pair Work: Make up a situational dialogue according to the information given below. Suppose you're planning a farewell party for your class. Now you are talking to the hotel receptionist to fix the details about the banquet. Make a dialogue with your partner based on the following information.

Details of the event:	Requests of services:	Decision on the menu:
A. Farewell party	A. A cake	A. Set Menu A
B. 30 people	B. Decoration with balloons	B. Changing some dishes
C. July 7th, 7 p.m.	C. Filming the event	C. 50 *Yuan* per head
D. Phone number	D. Karaoke	

B Translation

　i. Translate the following sentences into Chinese.

　　1. Clear entree plates, bread and butter plates, salt and pepper, and any surplus cutlery (餐具) not needed for dessert.
　　2. Place appetizers(开胃菜) on tables before service begins, unless they are hot items which must be served after the guests are seated.
　　3. Serve all plated food from the right, and serve anything that is actually passed by (传递) the guests from the left.

4. Generally, such similarities(相似性) occur because the rules established in dining areas are developed for a common purpose.

5. How many people are you planning to invite(邀请) and how much would you like to spend per person?

ii. Translate the following sentences into English.
1. 中餐宴会客人通常提前五至十分钟(5-10 minutes early)到达。
2. 进入宴会厅应脱大衣、脱帽、取下围巾(muffler) 和手套(glove)。
3. 宴会厅内宾客济济一堂,大厅里节日气氛(festive atmosphere)喜庆热烈。
4. 酒店西餐厅已经预订了。我们要安排(arrange)一个下周三的宴会。
5. 我们计划要来25人左右,每人不超过(no more than)20美元。

 Writing

Invitation Card 请柬

The invitation card is a most formal invitation letter, though very short in length, usually less than 14 lines. Due to its formality, the card would involve complete names instead of abbreviations, and salutation is very formal, for which Mr. and Mrs. are most preferred. In addition, the card is written in third person so that we do not use "I" or "we" in invitation cards.

When you're planning an event in the hotel, let guests know their presence. It is requested through an equally special invitation. Don't settle for generic store-bought invitation cards and you can make your own invitation card of the hotel.

Suppose you'll have a banquet in the hotel, write a dinner invitation card using the following example.

Outline:
1. Host: Mr. Tom Lance
2. Guests: Mr. John Smith and his family
3. Time: May 25th, 2020
4. Place: the second floor of Italian Restaurant
5. Name of the hotel: Intercontinental Hotel, Changchun

Example

A Dinner Invitation Card

> MR. AND MRS. ROBERT STANLEY
> REQUEST THE PLEASURE OF YOUR COMPANY
> AT DINNER
> THURSDAY, THE EIGHTH OF OCTOBER
> AT THIRTY AFTER SIX
> JINJIANG HOTEL
> CHANGSHA

Chapter 14
Recreational Activities
娱乐活动

Major Topics 一、酒店知识：What Is a Spa Hotel? 什么是温泉酒店？
二、酒店员工：Recreation Center Supervisor 康乐部主管
　　　　　　　Recreation Center Captain 康乐部领班
　　　　　　　Recreation Center Attendant 康乐部服务员
　　　　　　　Nightclub Manager 夜总会经理
三、酒店视频：How to Choose a Spa Resort? 怎么选择温泉度假胜地？
四、酒店对话：Scenario 1: Facilities and Programs 设施和项目
　　　　　　　Scenario 2: In the Gym 在健身馆
　　　　　　　Scenario 3: Sauna and Massage 桑拿和按摩
　　　　　　　Scenario 4: Taijiquan and Qigong 太极拳和气功
五、巩固练习

> This chapter concentrates on the recreational activities in a hotel. In *Part One*, you'll read ABC about a spa hotel as a warming-up exercise. In *Part Two*, job description of working staff is provided for you to have some basics about the responsibility of each job at Recreation Department. In *Part Three*, you'll watch a short video about the techniques of choosing a spa resort. In the next section, *Part Four* will provide some situational dialogues for you to practice the services for various recreational activities based on different scenarios. *Part Five* includes additional exercises to enhance your knowledge and skills of working as an attendant in the recreation center.

Part One ABC for Hotel
一、酒店知识

What Is a Spa Hotel? 什么是温泉酒店?

Word Tips

premium /ˈpriːmiəm/ n. 费用;保险费
yoga /ˈjəʊɡə/ n. 瑜伽
discount /ˈdɪskaʊnt/ n. 优惠,折价
top-notch /ˌtɒp ˈnɒtʃ/ adj. 拔尖的
fitness facilities /ˈfɪtnəs fəˈsɪlɪtɪz/ 健身器材

average /ˈævərɪdʒ/ adj. 平均
loyalty /ˈlɔɪəlti/ n. 忠诚
relaxation /ˌriːlækˈseɪʃn/ n. 放松;消遣
benefit /ˈbenɪfɪt/ n. 益处;好处
off-season /ˈɒf ˈsiːzn/ 淡季

  A spa hotel, also known as a hotel spa or an urban hotel spa, is usually found in big cities and major tourist and business destinations, such as New York City, Las Vegas, Washington D.C. and Los Angeles.

  A spa hotel typically offers luxurious and beautiful spa facilities, drama-like personal tea service, signature spa treatments you can't find anywhere else, and a higher level of amenities and customer service. In exchange, you pay a premium. Prices at spa hotels tend to be much higher than the average day spa. And the more luxurious the hotel and the spa, the higher the price.

  Spa hotels usually have facilities like steam, sauna, fitness facilities, and a swimming pool. Regular exercise classes are unusual, but some spa hotels have them. You might also be able to hire a personal trainer or yoga teacher for a private class.

  Spa hotels are open to locals as well as hotel guests. However, locals may not have full access to all the facilities a hotel guest would, like the pool or fitness facilities, or you may have to pay extra for a day pass. Make sure to ask if that's important to you. Sometimes spa hotels have special loyalty program for locals or offer discounts in off-season.

  Spa hotels are different from spa resorts (also known as resort spas), which offer outdoor recreation like golf, tennis, and swimming pools and sometimes even kids clubs. Both spa hotel and spa resorts are different from destination spas, also known as health spas, where the focus is on a healthy, engaged vacation full of exercise and spa cuisine.

  Spa hotels tend to have luxurious rooms, fine dining restaurants, and a luxurious spa that is all about rest and relaxation. It's a good choice when you're visiting a city, either as a tourist or a business traveler, and want top-notch spa treatments as part of the experience.

  To make the most of your time at a spa hotel, arrive at the spa 45 minutes or so in advance. This gives you plenty of time to get changes, shower, enjoy the amenities and atmosphere, and relax, so you're already relaxed when your treatment starts.

Give yourself time to rest after the spa treatment, to receive the full benefit. And if you're on business, book your treatment near the end of the day so you can go to bed right after.

Based on the above passage, decide whether the following statements are true or false. Write T for true and F for false.

1. _____ In spite of the luxurious amenities in spa hotels, you may not have the good treatments and customer service at spas elsewhere.
2. _____ It is a common practice for a spa hotel to offer regular exercise classes.
3. _____ Spa hotels receive locals, but may treat them differently from hotel guests.
4. _____ Hotel spas are different from both resort spas and destination spas.
5. _____ According to the passage, to enjoy the full benefit, you'd better spend most of your time at the spa hotel.

Part Two   Working Staff
二、酒店员工

1 Listen to the job description of each one in the department, correct the mistakes and put the right ones in the blanks.

(1) **Recreation Center Supervisor** is the head of the recreational department, who works with multiple sectors and makes sure that the recreation center is running properly. His major responsibilities are:

To supervise and coordinate the personnel administration, such as training staff and assigning work duties.

To oversee the daily operations of recreational facilities.

To maintain current equipment and order new equipment.

To supervise operations in different programs, collect customer complaints and improve work to promote sales.

 a. _____
 b. _____

中文提示：

　　康乐部主管 负责本部门的全面工作，协调各项目事务，保障康乐部正常运转。主要职责有：监督、协调人事管理，如员工培训、工作分配；监督康乐设施的日常运行；负责现有设备的维修和新设备的采购；督导不同项目的运行，收集顾客意见，改进工作，以增加销量。

(2) **Recreation Center Captain** reports to Recreation Center Supervisor, oversees the activities of staff to ensure quality service. His responsibilities are:

To organize day-to-day operations in the department, ensure safe use of facilities.

To create work programs and keep records of attendance.

To train staff about the rules and regulations of recreational facilities to maintain order and ensure safety of the equipment.

a. _____
b. _____

中文提示：

  康乐部领班 向康乐部主管汇报，监督员工工作，保证提供优质服务。其主要职责有：负责康乐部日常运营，保证设施安全使用；制订工作计划，监督员工考勤；培训员工遵守娱乐设施操作规范，确保设施正常运行、安全使用。

(3) **Recreation Center Attendant** reports to Recreation Center Captain, typically welcomes guests and works to ensure that guests have a safe and enjoyable experience. Their responsibilities are:

To observe job requirements, provide customers with excellent service.

To have a good knowledge of facility rules, and be polite in introducing to guests and demonstrate use of materials and equipment.

To be responsible for the examination and maintenance of facilities, ensuring they work properly.

To keep the equipment clean.

a. _____
b. _____

中文提示：

  康乐部服务员 向康乐部领班汇报；接待客人，保证客人尽兴、安全。其主要职责有：严格遵守工作规范，为顾客提供优质服务；熟悉各种器材的使用方法，耐心细致地向客人介绍，示范指导客人如何使用物品和设备；负责所属区域的设施设备的检查和保养，确保正常使用；保证设备清洁、干净。

(4) **Nightclub Manager** reports to the Manager of Recreation Department. The most important aspect of his job description is meeting expected sales quotas and profit margins for a nightclub. Other duties are:

To hire and train qualified employees, such as bartenders, barmaids, bouncers, cashiers, DJs, cooks and maintenance workers.

To oversee the process of all alcohol, food, ice, glasses, napkins and other supplies on a daily basis.

To entail planning and implementing special promotions.

To adhere to proper safety standards with regard to in-store operations, transferring cash to the bank and preventing skippers.

a. _____
b. _____

中文提示：

夜总会经理 向康乐部经理汇报；其最重要的职责是力争达到夜总会预期的销售额和边际利润，其他职责有：聘用和培训合格员工，如调酒师、吧员、保镖、收银员、流行音乐节目主持人、厨师、修理工等；每日督查所有酒类、菜品、杯具、餐巾和其他物品的供应；策划和实施特别促销；保证夜总会内部经营遵守安全标准，把现金存入银行以及防盗。

2 Listen again and discuss the job description of the post you wish to hold in your career.

Part Three　Video for the Hotel
三、酒店视频

How to Choose a Spa Resort? 怎样选择温泉度假胜地？

Word Tips

pleasurable /ˈpleʒərəbl/ adj. 愉快的
preference /ˈprefrəns/ n. 偏爱
brochure /ˈbrəʊʃʊə/ n. 手册
therapist /ˈθerəpɪst/ n. 治疗专家
nightingale /ˈnaɪtɪŋɡeɪl/ n. 夜莺
expertise /ˌekspɜːˈtiːz/ n. 专门知识

budget /ˈbʌdʒɪt/ n. 预算
facial /ˈfeɪʃl/ adj. 面部的
follow-up /ˈfɒləʊ ʌp/ n. 后续行动
geisha /ˈɡeɪʃə/ n. 艺妓
excrement /ˈekskrɪmənt/ n. 排泄物

A Watch the video twice, and fill in the blanks with the information you hear.

　　You can choose specific ala carte treatments at a (1) _____.

　　American spas are renowned for body treatments while European spas are for (2) _____.

　　When you find spas you're interested in (3) _____ the brochures, follow up with phone calls for prices and other options.

　　Gain a sense of expertise and atmosphere through web photos and (4) _____ conversations.

　　Find spas with therapists if you're seeking out therapeutic treatments. The better therapists tend to be found where spas are part of the (5) _____.

B Watch the video again, and answer the following questions.

1. What will you need when you select the spas?
   _____.

2. What are the six steps of choosing a spa?
   _____.

3. What are American spas famous for?
   _____.

4. What will you do when you find spas you're interested in?
   _____.

5. Where do the better therapists tend to be found?
   _____.

Part Four   Dialogues in the Hotel
四、酒店对话

Scenario 1

Facilities and Programs 设施和项目

A Listen to Dialogue 1. Pick up the items from Column B and put them under the corresponding categories in Column A.

Column A	Column B
1. Recreation Department:	A. nightclub B. dancing C. bowling room D. spring grips E. race apparatus
2. Nightclub:	F. Taiji Quan G. fashion show H. dumb bells I. gymnasium
3. Fitness Center:	G. swimming pool K. billiard room L. singing M. bar bells
4. Training Classes:	N. wall bars O. stationary bike P. aerobics

B Divide your class into groups of two or three students, and do the dialogue again.

G (Guest): People say that your hotel's Recreation Dept. is really fantastic. What do you have?

Receptionist (R): Well, we have a nightclub, a gym, a swimming pool, a bowling room, a billiard room, and so on.

G: What do you have in the nightclub?

R: In the night club, you can enjoy singing, dancing, fashion show, and so on.

G: Great! How about the fitness center?

R: It is equipped with the latest sports apparatus, such as the bar bells, dumb bells, spring grips, wall bars, race apparatus, stationary bike, you name it.

G: Terrific! I want to lose weight. Do you organize any training classes?

R: Yes, we have Taiji Quan and aerobics training classes.

G: One more thing, is there a coach who supervises the exercises?

R: Yes, over there you can see our resident coach.

Scenario 2

In the Gym 在健身馆

A Listen to Dialogue 2, and put the sentences in the correct order.

_____ **Jason (J):** But, gymnasium exercise seems a hard work for me.

_____ **Attendant (A):** Well, that depends on how you do it. Some people want to be in shape in a short time, so they overstress their bodies and can get hurt that way. But if you take it slowly and you won't.

_____ **J:** What kind of exercise can I do here?

_____ **A:** Have a try. I'll help you with it.

_____ **J:** I heard that intense exercise can hurt the muscles.

_____ **A:** Various things, like weight lifting, stretching, jogging on the treadmill and things like that.

_____ **J:** But it seems that other forms of exercise can also achieve the same results.

_____ **A:** Yes, they can. But in the gymnasium you have all the right equipment for different parts of your body. You can work out only your abdomen, biceps or triceps, or just build up your stamina.

B Role play: One student plays the role of attendant while another plays the role of Jason.

Scenario 3

> **Sauna and Massage 桑拿和按摩**

A Listen to Dialogue 3, and complete the following conversation with what you hear.

Attendant (A): Good afternoon, sir. Welcome.

Jason (J): Good afternoon. Where is my locker, please?

A: Would you hand me your key, sir? Your locker room is(1) _____ (*He takes the key, opens the locker and puts slippers on the floor for the guest.*)

J: Thank you very much. I'll have a sauna and (2)_____. By the way, what is the temperature in the sauna?

A: It's about 110 degrees centigrade. That's 212 Fahrenheit.

J: Where is the stove then?

A: There are (3)_____ near the door. They are electric. But don't worry. They are very safe. On top of the stoves, there are some stones.

J: OK. Is there any cold water in the sauna?

A: Yes. There is a wooden basin in the corner with cold water and (4)_____. Throw some water on the stones; the hot steam will immediately come out. With the steam increasing, your blood circulation will also increase.

J: Good. Now I know what to do. Thank you.

A: You are welcome. When you finish your sauna, you can take (5)_____ in the after-sauna room.

J: Thanks. I'll see you later.

A: See you later. Enjoy it.

B Listen to the dialogue again, and do a situational dialogue with your partner.

Scenario 4

> **Taijiquan and Qigong 太极拳和气功**

A Listen to Dialogue 4 and decide whether the following statements are true or false. Write T for true and F for false.

_____ 1. The guest asks the clerk to recommend some modern Chinese exercise for him.

_____ 2. Qigong, a latest Chinese boxing, is an important branch of Chinese martial arts.

_____ 3. The movement of Taijiquan is even and slow. It is used for life enhancement and health building.

_____ 4. Qigong is a kind of breathing exercise which originates from yoga.

_____ 5. A resident coach will stand by to show the trainees exactly what to do.

B Listen to the dialogue again and answer the following questions.

1. What does the guest inquire about?
   _____.

2. What alias does Chinese Taijiquan have?
   _____.

3. Is the Indian yoga similar with Chinese breathing exercise?
   _____.

4. Where does the guest get registered for his training class?
   _____.

Clerk (C): Good evening, sir. Welcome to our Fitness Center. How may I help you?
Guest (G): I want to do some exercises. Could you recommend some traditional Chinese exercise for me?
C: Have you ever heard of Taijiquan or Qigong exercises?
G: What is Taijiquan?
C: We also call it Chinese Shadow Boxing. It's an important branch of Chinese martial arts. The movement is even and slow. It's used for life enhancement and health building. Many Chinese are fond of it.
G: I see. And what about Qigong?
C: Qigong is a kind of breathing exercise.
G: Is it similar to yoga?
C: You are right. Which one do you prefer, Taijiquan or Qigong?
G: Do you have a coach here to supervise the exercise?
C: Yes, we have a resident coach standing by to show you exactly what to do. If you need any help or instructions, just call him.
G: Ok. I think I'll get registered in your Taijiquan training class.

Additional Exercises:

Divide the class into groups. Each group makes a situational dialogue using words or phrases for the Recreational Activities. You may refer to the working procedures or sentence patterns in Dialogue 1, Dialogue 2, Dialogue 3 and Dialogue 4.

Additional Words and Phrases 更多的词汇短语储备

Word Tips

tennis court 网球场	karaoke bar 卡拉Ok酒吧
billiards room 台球室	recumbent cycle 斜靠式脚踏器
ballroom 舞厅	rowing machine 划船器
bowling room 保龄球馆	chest expander 扩胸器
beauty parlor 美容院	physician scale 体重秤
cross trainer 运转器	aerobic stair climber 爬楼器

Part Five Consolidation
五、巩固练习

A Match the terms in column A with the meanings in column B.

Column A	Column B
A. body care service	a. 保健服务
B. bathing service	b. 射箭
C. health care service	c. 沙狐球
D. entertainment service	d. 香草泡浴
E. arrow shooting	e. 娱乐服务
F. medical examinations	f. 洗浴服务
G. recreational facilities	d. 体检
H. shuffle board	e. 康体服务
I. fragrant herbal bath	f. 康乐设施

B Translation

i. Translate the following sentences into Chinese.

1. Facilities at the hotel also include a fully equipped spa, fitness centre, sauna, floodlit (泛光灯照明) outdoor tennis court, and a 20 meter indoor heated swimming pool.
2. The fifth floor of the hotel will feature a landscaped roof garden including an outdoor heated swimming pool, a terrace and Jacuzzi (按摩池) with sundeck.
3. Our gymnasium is well-equipped with all the latest sports apparatus (运动器材), some of which integrates the amusement and the body building.
4. Taijiquan is an important branch of Chinese martial arts, which is used for life enhancement (延年益寿) and health building.

5. I hate watching something boring on TV in the room. Is there any place in the hotel where we can amuse (娱乐) ourselves?

ii. Translate the following sentences into English.
1. 地下室有一个娱乐中心，你可以去打台球、乒乓球、桥牌(bridge)、保龄球(bowling)。
2. 请问水的温度(temperature)是多少？游泳池水深是多少米？
3. 办理健身会员卡(member card)30次，700元，有效期为三个月。
4. 更衣室在那边。男更衣室(gentlemen's) 在左边，女更衣室(lady's) 在右边。
5. 你需要换好运动鞋和健身服(workout clothes)才可以到健身房运动。

C Writing

Bulletin Board 公告牌

A bulletin board (pinboard, pin board, noticeboard, or notice board in British English) is a surface intended for the posting of public messages, for example, to advertise items wanted or for sale, announce events, or provide information. Bulletin boards are often made of a material such as cork to facilitate addition and removal of messages, or they can be placed on computer networks so people can leave and erase messages for other people to read and see. A vividly decorated bulletin board is sure to draw many hotel guests to the recreational activities of your hotel.

Suppose you are the manager of Recreational Department and you want to achieve your sales target, make a bulletin board to promote a show which is to be held in the nightclub of your hotel.

Outline:
1. Time
2. Place
3. Performers
4. DJ
5. Entrance fees
6. Ways of ticket booking

Chapter 15

Shopping Arcade
购物中心

Major Topics 一、酒店知识：The FUD Factor: How to Persuade Customers to Buy? FUD 因素：怎样才能说服顾客购买?
二、酒店员工：Store Manager 商场部经理
Assistant Manager 商场部副经理
Sales Assistant 商场营业员
Store Cashier 商场收银员
三、酒店视频：Safety Instructions about Online Shopping 网上购物安全须知
四、酒店对话：Scenario 1: Inquiring about Customers' Preferences 询问偏好
Scenario 2: Recommending Specialties 推荐特产
Scenario 3: Talking about Prices 商谈价格
Scenario 4: Packaging 包装礼品
五、巩固练习

This chapter centers on the topic of shopping in the hotel. In *Part One*, you'll read an article about sales promotion: The FUD Factor: How to Persuade Customers to Buy. In *Part Two*, job description of working staff is provided for you to have some basics about the responsibility of each job in a shopping arcade. In *Part Three*, you'll watch a short video regarding the safety instructions about online shopping. In the next section, *Part Four* will provide some situational dialogues for you to practice skills of the shop assistant based on different scenarios. *Part Five* includes additional exercises to enhance your knowledge and skills of working in a shopping arcade and enhance your English abilities and skills of promoting sales.

Part One ABC for Hotel
一、酒店知识

The FUD Factor: How to Persuade Customers to Buy? FUD因素：怎样才能说服顾客购买？

Word Tips

entrepreneur /ˌɒntrəprəˈnɜː(r)/ n. 企业家；主办人
mousetrap /ˈmaʊstræp/ n. 捕鼠器
innovative /ˈɪnəveɪtɪv/ adj. 革新的；创新的
substitution /ˌsʌbstɪˈtjuːʃn/ n. 代替；代用
warranty /ˈwɒrənti/ n. 保证书
perception /pəˈsepʃn/ n. 觉察（力）；观念
persuade /pəˈsweɪd/ v. 说服，劝说
astray /əˈstreɪ/ adv. 误入歧途地
disillusioned /ˌdɪsɪˈluːʒnd/ adj. 幻想破灭的
approach /əˈprəʊtʃ/ v. 接近，走近
guarantee /ˌɡærənˈtiː/ v. 保证，担保
visualize /ˈvɪʒuəlaɪz/ v. 设想；使可见
intangible /ɪnˈtændʒəbl/ adj. 难以理解的；无法确定的

Ralph Waldo Emerson, the great 19th-century American writer, has led many an entrepreneur astray with his famous saying: "If you build a better mousetrap, the world will beat a path to your door." Therein lies many a disillusioned entrepreneur and failed company. Entrepreneurs who sit and wait for the customers to come to them wind up sitting and waiting while the world passes them by. The only entrepreneurs who succeed are those who beat a path to the world.

Smart entrepreneurs know something about human psychology and appreciate the hesitation that customers can feel when dealing with a new company or considering the purchase of an innovative product or service. Consequently, to help customers understand the benefits of their products or services, entrepreneurs must first learn and respect the customers' state of mind. If they do, they can take an approach to dealing with customers that is neither technical nor fancy. It just works!

Successful entrepreneurs make use of FUD to their advantage. FUD stands for Fear, Uncertainty and Doubt. Most customers tend to have a high degree of FUD when considering whether to do business with a new company about which they may know little or nothing. Consequently, entrepreneurs need to reduce FUD in the minds of customers. They do this in a variety of ways.

Justify the cost of the product or service, to the customer. This may require preparing a cost-benefit analysis and justifying the substitution cost of replacing what they are currently using with your product or service.

Stress the benefits of the product or service rather than its features—that is, how it helps the customer, rather than what it does. Show how the product or service meets a customer need or solves a problem, instead of describing how the product or service operates.

Provide support. Reinforce a purchase decision by providing guarantees, warranties and training.

Demonstrate. Actually show the product or service, to remove any questions that it actually does what you say it will do. The ability to prove a product, visualize a value and illustrate intangibles is a powerful way to reduce FUD.

These approaches indicate that entrepreneurs must understand the worries, issues and perceptions of customers and be aware of the power of FUD in the customer's mind. By developing products and services that meet real needs and solve real problems, you can overcome the Fear, Uncertainty and Doubt that customers may have. By appreciating the very real concerns that customers feel, you can choose approaches to decrease FUD and effectively persuade customers to see the Fun, Usefulness and Delight of your products and services, an alternative interpretation of FUD.

Based on the above passage, decide whether the following statements are true or false. Write T for true and F for false.

1. _____ Emerson's saying has benefited many entrepreneurs and helped them to do successful business.
2. _____ According to the author, understanding the customers' psychology is the first step of persuading them to buy.
3. _____ When explaining a product, the businessman should focus the customer's attention on how the product works.
4. _____ Illustrating a product will help convince the customer about the functions claimed by the entrepreneur.
5. _____ FUD in this passage can be interpreted in two different ways.

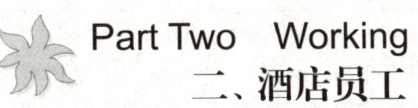

Part Two Working Staff
二、酒店员工

1 Listen to the job description of each one in the department, correct the mistakes and put the right ones in the blanks.

(1) **Store Manager** is the head of the store, who manages the sales, operational and personnel functions of the store to ensure best profits. Some of the responsibilities are:

To effectively manage employee flow and develop action plans for employee sales growth.
To monitor supply levels.
To conduct inventories / maintain inventory records.
To promptly and accurately complete all paperwork procedures.

a. _____
b. _____

中文提示：

　　商场部经理 负责商场销售、运营及人事工作，保证商场获取最大销售利润。其主要职责有：有效控制员工流动，促进销售业绩增长；保障货源，盘点库存，建立商品目录；及时、准确处理日常文件。

(2) **Assistant Manager** reports to Store Manager, responsible for assisting with the day-to-day management and operations. His major responsibilities are:

To conduct floor cleaning and maintain adequate sales.
To assist in the inventory and maintenance of inventory records.
To conduct presentations, provide quality product demonstrations.
To handle customer complaint, develop strong customer relationship.

a. _____
b. _____

中文提示：

　　商场部副经理 向商场部经理汇报，协助日常管理和销售工作。主要职责有：清洁卖场，保持充分销量；协助盘点库存，清理商品目录；陈列商品，展示优质产品；处理客人投诉，与客人建立牢固关系。

(3) **Sales Assistant** conducts the daily operations of the store and the daily activities of the sales to promote products to ensure customer satisfaction. Their responsibilities are:

To manage inventory.
To maintain a neat and tidy store logo.
To be informed of the product standard and information.
To identify customer needs and direct them to an appropriate product.

a. _____
b. _____

中文提示：

　　商场营业员 承担日常销售工作，产品促销，确保顾客满意。其主要职责有：整理商品库存，掌握销售情况；保持店招整洁；熟悉商品种类、规格、特点等信息；了解顾客需求，帮助顾客选择合适的产品。

(4) **Store Cashier** may perform a wide range of job duties. Key responsibilities include:

To complete customer transactions.
To handle money.
Cashiers at large stores may work exclusively on the cash register. At other stores, cashiers may perform a number of additional responsibilities, including processing refunds, answering phones, wrapping gifts, packaging goods, and signing members up for rewards cards.

a. _____
b. _____

中文提示：

商场收银员 主要职责是完成顾客交易，管好钱。大型商场收银员只负责收银；其他商店收银员可能还会承担其他工作，如处理退货、接电话、包装礼品、货物装袋、发放促销卡等。

2 Listen again and discuss the job description of the post you wish to hold in your career.

Part Three Video for the Hotel
三、酒店视频

Safety Instructions about Online Shopping 网上购物安全须知

Word Tips

purchase /ˈpɜːtʃəs/ n. 购买
review /rɪˈvjuː/ n. 评论
overstock /ˌəʊvəˈstɒk/ v. 库存过剩
reputation /ˌrepjuˈteɪʃn/ n. 名气，名声
obviously /ˈɒbvɪəslɪ/ adj. 明显地

credible /ˈkredəbl/ adj. 可信的
website /ˈwebsaɪt/ n. 网站
rating /ˈreɪtɪŋ/ n. 等级；评估
homepage n. 主页

A Watch the video twice, and decide whether the following statements are True or False.

1. _____ Clicking on seller ratings, you can read people's comments on the quality of the products they have bought on a website.
2. _____ According to the speaker, Amazon.com does not have a good reputation for customer service.
3. _____ You can usually find the privacy policy of a website at the top right corner of its homepage.
4. _____ Privacy policy of a website informs the site users how their personal information will be used.
5. _____ The purpose of this video episode is to instruct the online shoppers how to make sure the website on which they buy things is trustworthy.

B Watch the video again, and answer the following questions.

1. What can you learn from the video?
   _____.

2. How can you get the reviews that other people have left about the site that you are browsing?
   _____.

3. Why is the seller rating very important for the online shopping?
   _____.

4. Where can you usually find the privacy policy about a website?
   _____.

5. If you want to make sure you're protected for your online shopping, what do you need to do?
   _____.

Part Four   Dialogues in the Hotel
四、酒店对话

Scenario 1

Inquiring about Customers' Preferences 询问偏好

A Listen to Dialogue 1, and complete the following conversation with what you hear.

Shop assistant (A): Good morning, madam. Anything I can do for you?
Jane (J): I supposed I'd like to buy something as (1) _____ for my husband and daughter.
A: What about some (2) _____ for your husband?
J: Oh, no. I bought one for him as a birthday present last month.
A: What about these T-shirts (3) _____?
J: That's a good idea. Could you show me some samples?
A: My pleasure. They're of good quality.
J: I prefer a light color, (4) _____.
A: How about this white one?
J: It's really nice. How much does it cost?
A: $14.
J: OK. I'll take it. Could you recommend something (5) _____?
A: We've got very beautiful silk products and woolen sweaters.
J: The woolen sweaters are (6) _____ because it is getting warm. How much are these green pajamas?

A: $17.

J: They are too expensive. I wonder if the silk piece's color will fade.

A: As a matter of fact, all the materials here are (7) _____. If you are not satisfied with the price, you can try a silk scarf. It is just $12.

J: All right. I will buy a white T-shirt, and (8) _____. I think green is my daughter's favorite.

A: That amounts to $26. Please wash the silk in (9) _____ soap water and rinse well. Don't rub or (10) _____ it.

J: Here is the money. Thank you.

A: You're welcome.

B Divide your class into groups of two or three students, and do the dialogue again.

Scenario 2

Recommending Specialties 推荐特产

A Listen to Dialogue 2 and decide whether the following statements are True or False.

(1) _____ The guest is on holiday, and wants to buy some presents for her daughter.

(2) _____ The shop assistant recommends a Chinese liquor as the souvenir.

(3) _____ Longjing tea is a kind of green tea, which is very famous in China.

(4) _____ The shop assistant suggests the guest should buy a tea caddy to keep the tea in.

(5) _____ The guest pays the bill by cash because her credit card does not work.

B Role play: One student plays the role of a shop assistant while another plays the role of a guest.

Jane (J): Hello. I'd like to buy some tea.

Shop Assistant (A): What kind of tea would you like?

J: I don't know. I'm here on holiday and it will be a gift for my sister.

A: In England black tea is very popular but in China most people drink green tea. You should buy some green tea as a souvenir.

J: OK. Which tea do you recommend?

A: We have many varieties of tea that you can try. My favorite is Longjing tea. It's a famous green tea.

J: Can I try some?

A: Yes, here you are.

J: That tastes lovely. It's very drinkable.

A: Yes, it's very refreshing. Would you like to buy some?

J: Yes. What other souvenirs can you recommend?
A: You should buy a tea caddy to keep the tea in.
J: OK. What else?
A: How about a thermos to keep the tea warm?
J: Good idea, I'll take one. How much does this all cost?
A: That comes to 550 RMB.
J: OK, here's my credit card.

Scenario 3

Talking about Prices 商谈价格

A Listen to Dialogue 3, and complete the table with what you hear.

No.	Souvenirs	Accept(A)/Refuse(R)	Reasons
1	ring		
2	bracelet		
3	gold pen		
4	watch		
5	hat		

B Listen to the dialogue again, and do the dialogue again with your partner.

Shop Assistant (A): Can I help you, sir?
Jason (J): Yes, I need something for my daughter. It's her birthday, so I want something special.
A: Well, how much do you want to spend?
J: Oh, money doesn't matter.
A: Oh? Well, how about a nice ring?
J: That's a good idea. Mmm... how much is this one?
A: That's, er, $1,259.
J: Oh, er, not quite the right design for my daughter.
A: Well, here's a beautiful bracelet. It's only $545. It's eighteen carat gold.
J: Hmm. Well... no, that's not quite right. I don't like the shape.
A: I know. How about this gold pen? It's only $135, and it will last forever!
J: Mmm. No, no, I don't think so. Oh, dear, it's much too heavy!
A: Too heavy! I see. Well, how about a watch?

J: How much is your cheapest watch?

A: Let's see. Oh, here's one for, er, $23.75—that's twenty three dollars and seventy-five cents.

J: Ah. No. I don't think she would like that watch. It's too big! Ah ha! How about that hat over there?

A: The hat? But I thought you wanted...

J: Oh, it's beautiful! How much is it?

A: It's, er, $2.85.

J: It's perfect! I'll take it! She'll love it!

Scenario 4

Packaging 包装礼品

A Listen to Dialogue 4, and put the sentences in the correct order and act it out with your partner.

_____ **Shop assistant(S):** My pleasure. Please handle with care. Don't put it upside down.

_____ **S:** Please check the goods in the package. Will that do?

_____ **S:** Don't worry, madam. I'll wrap them up for you and send them to your room.

_____ **S:** Is there anything else you are interested in?

_____ **Mrs. Bellow(B):** Oh, don't bother, please. I'll manage if you wrap things up for me. Do you have Zhangfei Beef? I had some at my Chinese friend's home. It's good.

_____ **S:** Take it easy, madam. I'll manage it.

_____ **B:** OK. Get me 2 bags.

_____ **S:** Here you are. Now, let the jars go into the carton with some soft paper filled in between. Let me put the beef in the big plastic bag.

_____ **B:** That's very thoughtful of you.

_____ **B:** What's more important, I fear the chinaware I bought might be broken.

_____ **B:** Yes, I'd love to have some other Sichuan specialties, but I'm afraid I won't be able to carry so many things in the bags.

_____ **B:** Take care! The porcelains are fragile.

_____ **S:** Yes, we do. It's a famous Sichuan specialty, and it's always good to bring along for your journey.

B Listen to the dialogue again, and answer the following questions.

1. What does the guest want to buy as a souvenir?

_____.

2. What does the guest worry about?

_____.

3. How does the shop assistant protect porcelains when she puts them in the carton?
   _____.
4. What does the shop assistant advise the guest to do when carrying the carton?
   _____.

Additional Exercises:

Divide the class into groups. Each group makes a situational dialogue using words or phrases for the Shopping Arcade. You may refer to the working procedures or sentence patterns in Dialogue 1, Dialogue 2, Dialogue 3 and Dialogue 4.

Additional Words and Phrases 更多的词汇短语储备

Word Tips

bracelet 手镯	fancy lantern 彩灯
Chinese chess 象棋	cloisonné 景泰蓝
cheongsam 旗袍	silhouette carving 影雕
Tangkha painting 唐卡	clay figurine 泥人
New Year pictures 年画	lacquerware 漆器
abacus 算盘	porcelain 瓷器

Part Five   Consolidation
五、巩固练习

A Read the following advertisements, and choose the best answer to each of the statements.

HOTEL SHOPS

In our luxury hotel lobby, you will find a variety of shops ranging from home entertainment systems to upscale jewelry. They are:

Bang & Olufsen

Founded in 1925, Bang & Olufsen is built on more than 80 years of Danish craftsmanship and innovation. The brand is world-renowned for its highly distinctive and exclusive range of televisions, music systems, loudspeakers, telephones and multimedia products, combining technological excellence with emotional appeal.

Davidoff

Davidoff carries a large assortment of high-end lifestyle accessories for men, such as Zino cutters, Corini Lamborghini cufflinks and many other interesting handmade products from the Dominican Republic and Cuba.

Hours:
Mondays to Saturdays: 11:00am to 8:30pm
Sundays and public holidays: 12:00 noon to 7:00pm
Tel: 6737 7500

Hours : 11:00am to 10:00pm daily
Tel : 6235 7921

Lavaliere

A contemporary boutique that is synonymous with fine jewellery, exquisite designs and exceptional craftsmanship.

Royal Insignia

Royal Insignia believe in the design philosophy that every piece of their creation must be of high artistic excellence that is inspired by passion and creativity. Their hand-crafted fine jewellery pieces are meant to be enjoyed for a lifetime.

Hours: 10:30am to 8:00pm daily
Tel: 6732 6693

Hours:
Mondays to Fridays: 10:30am to 7:30pm
Saturdays: 10:00am to 7:00pm
Sundays : closed
Tel: 7328 3456

1. If you want to buy a shaver for your father or boyfriend, you'd better go to _____.
    a) Bang & Olufsen
    b) Davidoff
    c) Lavaliere
    d) Royal Insignia

2. To get more information about jewellery pieces on Sundays, you should check with the shop by calling _____.
    a) 6737 7500
    b) 6235 7921
    c) 6732 6693
    d) 7328 3456

3. At Bang & Olufsen, you're likely to buy some _____ for your family.
    a) electrical devices
    b) facial products
    c) men's accessories
    d) fine jewellery

B Translation

i. Translate the following sentences into Chinese.

1. How do you like this one? The background is pale blue(浅蓝色)with traditional Chinese paintings of mountains and rivers.

2. Tell us a little bit about what you want. We have all shapes, sizes, qualities(品质), and price range.

3. May I have a close look at these cheongsams(旗袍)? I can't decide which one I like

better.

4. We just received a shipment of handbags of several different styles(各式各样). You have a lot of choices.

5. I just look for something for my husband. What would you recommend(推荐)?

ii. Translate the following sentences into English.

1. 您到这边来看看好吗,女士? 这里有一些漂亮的腰带,它们都是用袋鼠(kangaroos)皮或是鳄鱼(crocodiles)皮做的。
2. 这是当前最流行的款式,因为简洁,所以很好搭配(go with)衣服。
3. 我的性格有些保守(conservative)。你说我该选哪个好?
4. 我们的产品是经过抗过敏(anti-allergic)测验的,适合任何肤质。
5. 这款香奈儿(Chanel)的裙子怎么样? 这是我们销售最好(biggest sellers)的商品之一。

C Writing

Recruitment 招聘启事

Creating effective recruitment advertising can help a hotel attract qualified, motivated and skilled applicants. Long-term effects of solid recruitment and selection processes are strong employee performance, low turnover and high retention levels of a hotel. When you recruit an employee you should list the differences between required qualifications and preferred qualifications.

Suppose you're the manager of shopping arcade in a five-star hotel and you're ready to recruit a shop assistant, write an employment advertisement which lists the following requirements:

Outline:

1. Having good interpersonal skills
2. Ability to work well as part of a team
3. Having a polite and helpful manner
4. Being numerate to deal with money on a daily basis
5. Working overtime at weekends

Chapter 16
Complaints Settlement
处理投诉

Major Topics 一、酒店知识：Why Do Hotel Guests Complain? 为什么酒店客人要投诉？
二、酒店员工：Reception Supervisor 接待主管
Receptionist 接待员
三、酒店视频：A Complaint in the Hotel Restaurant 酒店餐厅里的投诉
四、酒店对话：Scenario 1: Complaint about the Food Quality 菜品质量投诉
Scenario 2: Complaint about Poor Service 服务质量投诉
Scenario 3: Complaint about Luggage Delivery 行李交送投诉
Scenario 4: Complaint about a Mistake in a Reservation 预订错误投诉

五、巩固练习

> This chapter concentrates on the topic of dealing with hotel guest complaints. In *Part One*, you'll read ABC about hotel guest complaints and the reasons why they complain. In *Part Two*, job description of working staff is provided for you to have some basics about the responsibility of each job in the departments of a hotel. In *Part Three*, you'll watch a short video about complaining in a restaurant. In the next section, *Part Four* will provide some situational dialogues for you to practice skills of handling complaints based on different scenarios. *Part Five* includes additional exercises to enhance your skills of dealing with complaints that you may encounter in your career.

Part One ABC for Hotel
一、酒店知识

Why Do Hotel Guests Complain? 为什么酒店客人要投诉？

Word Tips

illumination /ɪˌluːmɪˈneɪʃn/ *n.* 照明；阐明
concrete /ˈkɒŋkriːt/ *adj.* 具体的，有形的
indifferent /ɪnˈdɪfrənt/ *adj.* 漠不关心的
enrich /ɪnˈrɪtʃ/ *v.* 使充实，使富有
investigate /ɪnˈvestɪgeɪt/ *v.* 调查；审查
irresponsible /ˌɪrɪˈspɒnsəbl/ *adj.* 不负责任的
reinforce /ˌriːɪnˈfɔːs/ *v.* 加固，使更结实
handle /ˈhændl/ *v.* 操作，操控

Guest complaints can be classified into 4 kinds: complaint about equipment, complaint about service attitude, complaint about hotel service quality, and complaint about unexpected events.

The equipment can include air-conditioner, illumination, water supply, power supply, furniture, elevator and so on. Dealing with these complaints, the best way for the receptionists in the front office is first to investigate on the spot, then to take measures according to the concrete situation. After that, the receptionist should telephone the guest to make sure if the guest is satisfied.

The complaints about service attitude generally focus on the following: rude language, irresponsible reply, icy manner, indifferent manner, or with respective characters, the complaints happen very easily.

The third include that an attendant does not follow the principle of "first come, first served" in serving the guest, distributes the wrong room, not delivering the mails to guests in time, not carrying the luggage for guests, and not giving morning call on time, etc. The best way to reduce complaints is to reinforce the training on service clerks. It's necessary to train them in establishing a correct attitude to the guest, enriching their knowledge and improving their skills.

The last kind is that the hotel cannot help guests buy tickets or train tickets, the flight is not on time because of the weather, or the rooms are sold out, all belong to unexpected events, about which guests may complain. It's difficult for the hotel to handle such complaints, but guests hope that the hotel can help them to solve the problems. The receptionists should try their best to help solve the problems, and if they cannot, they should explain it clearly to the guests. Most guests can understand completely, as long as the servers are showing good sense.

Based on the above passage, decide whether the following statements are true or false. Write T for true and F for false.

1. _____ Dealing with complaints about equipment, the best way for the receptionists in the front office is first to take measures according to the concrete situation.
2. _____ The complaints about service attitude only focus on rude language and irresponsible reply.
3. _____ The third kind of complaints includes that an attendant does not follow the principle of "first come, first served."
4. _____ It's difficult to handle complaints about unexpected events, for guests hope that the hotel can help them to solve the problems.
5. _____ Most guests can understand completely, as long as the servers are showing good sense.

Part Two Working Staff
二、酒店员工

1 Listen to the job description of each one in the department, correct the mistakes and put the right ones in the blanks.

(1) **Reception Supervisor** reports to Reception Manager, makes sure the operations run smoothly. The responsibilities are:

To supervise Front Desk operations during holidays to a consistently high standard.

To monitor the standards and performance of team members with an emphasis on training and team work.

To deal with guest problems and complaints promptly and efficiently.

a. _____
b. _____

中文提示：

接待主管 向接待经理汇报，确保接待工作正常运行。其职责有：监督节假日期间前台的换班工作，保证高标准服务；做好员工培训，强调团队精神，考核绩效；回答客人咨询，快速有效处理投诉。

(2) **Receptionist** provides reception service to every guest. The responsibilities are:

To be ready to provide service for guest registration and departure.

To settle guest disputes, and ensure the bill accurate.

To maintain accurate guest accounts.

To answer and handle queries in a professional and profitable way.

a. _____
b. _____

中文提示：

　　接待员 为每一位客人提供服务。主要职责有：准备接待客人，登记入住，办理离店手续；处理纠纷，确保账单无误；准确记录家人信息；专业有礼地回答、处理客人诉求。

2 Listen again and discuss the job description of the post you wish to hold in your career.

Part Three　Video for the Hotel
三、酒店视频

A Complaint in the Hotel Restaurant 酒店餐厅里的投诉

Word Tips

righteous /ˈraɪtʃəs/ adj. 正义的
sprinkling /ˈsprɪŋklɪŋ/ n. 少量；点滴
inedible /ɪnˈedəbl/ adj. 不能吃的
compensation /ˌkɒmpenˈseɪʃn/ n. 赔偿；补偿
aversion /əˈvɜːʒn, -ʃən/ n. 厌恶；讨厌的人
complementary /ˌkɒmplɪˈmentri/ adj. 免费的
fobbed off 被欺骗

indignation /ˌɪndɪgˈneɪʃn/ n. 愤慨，愤怒
fuss /fʌs/ n. 大惊小怪
replacement /rɪˈpleɪsmənt/ n. 更换；代替
allergy /ˈælədʒi/ n. 过敏
aggressive /əˈgresɪv/ adj. 好斗的
poison /ˈpɔɪzn/ v. 使中毒

A Watch the video twice, and decide whether the following statements are true or false according to the video.

1. _____ It is too late to complain when you've eaten half of an inedible meal or if the bill is put on your table.
2. _____ You may remove money off the bill or expect a replacement meal or probably leave without being charged.
3. _____ It is worth telling the waiter of any allergies to particular ingredients while you're ordering.
4. _____ You may replace your food if you are aggressive with the waiter for the bad food.
5. _____ A tip is necessary if the waiter gave you a discount or complimentary dish though the food was not good enough.

6. _____ Complaint and compliment are equally important to the customer service and hotel management.

B Watch the video again, and answer the following questions.

1. How do you understand "Identify your aims" when you complain in the restaurant?
   _____.
2. If a meal is served as described on the menu, can the customer ask for change of the food?
   _____.
3. How does a customer solve the problem if the complaint cannot be solved with the waiter or waitress?
   _____.
4. What would a customer do if he left a restaurant and became seriously ill?
   _____.
5. Why does the restaurant manager always appreciate feedbacks from the customers?
   _____.

Part Four   Dialogues in the Hotel
四、酒店对话

Scenario 1

Complaint about the Food Quality 菜品质量投诉

A Listen to Dialogue 1, and complete the following conversation with what you hear.

Peter:(P) Excuse me, miss?
Waitress:(W) Yes, sir. What can I do for you?
P: I'm afraid they have put the wrong dressing (1)_____. This is Ranch Dressing, and I want Thousand Island.
W: Oh, I'm awfully sorry. I'll get you another one.
P: Thank you. And can you get me (2)_____? I don't have one here. And my finger is not that clean.
W: Sure! I'm so sorry, sir. Sometimes when we are in a hurry, we might make (3)_____. I'd be back with it right now.
P: Thanks! Listen, I really hate to (4)_____, but my chicken is too tough. I tried but I really cannot take this.
W: Oh, I'm terribly sorry, sir. I'll send it back to the kitchen. I can bring you something else if you like.

P: Thank you. I think I'm (5)_____. Can I have my bill?

W: Sure, Sir. We're so sorry about what happened. And we'll offer you a 50% (6)_____. Hope to see you again.

P: Well, we'll see.

B Divide your class into a group of two or three students, and do the dialogue again.

Scenario 2

Complaint about Poor Service 服务质量投诉

A Listen to Dialogue 2 and answer the following questions.

1. Why do the customers ask to change the table?

2. Do you think the customers are thirsty? What do they ask the waiter for?

3. How long have they been waiting for the refill?

4. What else are they still short of?

5. What do they ask the waiter to bring in the end?

B Listen to the dialogue again, and make a situational dialogue with your partner based on the following:

No.	Waiter	Customer
1	to change your soup	Your soup is cold and salty.
2	to send the dish back to kitchen	Your beef is overdone.
3	to apologize for the mistake	They send you something that you didn't order.
4	to request the man lower his voice	The man at the nearby table keeps talking loudly on his cell phone.
5	to offer discount as compensation	to express disappointment about this dining experience

Jason (J): By the way, could you move us to that window table? This part is a bit noisy than we expected, and we prefer somewhere quiet.

Waitress (W): Sure, sir. Let me check the window table first. Excuse me for a moment, sir.

J: Well, she seems to forget us. I can't see her anymore. Then, I have to be the bad guy. Excuse me. Can you refill our water glasses please?

Waiter:	Yes, sir. Anyone helps you? I'm sorry. I'll be right back with iced water.
J:	Listen. We've been waiting for more than half an hour for the refill. But no one came. We asked to move to the window table, but the waitress just totally forgot us. And, as you may notice, we are still short of a set of knife and fork, which we have asked for at least twice.
Waiter:	I'm terribly sorry for what happened. We have a huge dinner party tonight.
J:	I understand, but can you bring us some bread first? We're starving.
Waiter:	Sorry, sir. I'll go to check your order and be back with iced water, bread, knife and fork.

Scenario 3

Complaint about Luggage Delivery 行李交送投诉

A Listen to Dialogue 3 and complete the table with what you hear.

Name of the Guest	
Room Number	
Pieces of Luggage	
Colors of Suitcases	
Nametag (Yes/No)	

B Listen to the dialogue again, write numbers in the blanks to show the correct order of the dialogue and act it out with your partner.

_____	**Bell service (S):**	Good afternoon. Bell service. Can I help you?
_____	**Guest (G):**	Yes, I checked in half an hour ago. Why hasn't my luggage been sent up yet?
_____	**S:**	Is your nametag attached to it?
_____	**G:**	How long need I wait for it?
_____	**S:**	I'm sorry, sir. May I know your name and room number, please?
_____	**G:**	Thank you.
_____	**S:**	I'm sorry, Mr. Bluster. Two travel groups were checking in this afternoon, and the luggage has to be sent one floor at a time.
_____	**S:**	Don't worry, Mr. Bluster. I'll check them for you. Would you please give me some feature of your luggage?
_____	**S:**	You're welcome.
_____	**S:**	Just wait a moment, please. Mr. Bluster, I'm sorry to have kept you waiting. Your luggage is already on the way.

	G:	Tom Bluster, Room 1226.
	G:	Certainly. I have three bags. One is a small black suitcase and the other two are brown suitcases.
	S:	Yes, sir.

Scenario 4

Complaint about a Mistake in a Reservation 预订错误投诉

A Listen to Dialogue 4 and decide whether the following statements are true or false according to the dialogue.

1. _____ The guest would like to have a party in a hotel. She booked a table for more than three people.
2. _____ There was no table reservation marked in the name of Reynolds. It was the guest who probably forgot the reservation.
3. _____ The guest said she was promised a window table when she called the hotel yesterday afternoon.
4. _____ Another window table was offered to the guest as the guest requested.
5. _____ The guest was happy that the hotel would make efforts to make the party a pleasant one.

B Listen to the dialogue again and answer the following questions.

1. For how many people did Reynolds reserve the table?
   _____.
2. What was the problem about her reservation?
   _____.
3. What did the hotel promise to offer to Reynolds?
   _____.
4. How did the hotel staff apologize to Reynolds?
   _____.

Staff (S): Good evening, madam. For how many people?
Reynolds (R): A party of four.
S: Do you have a reservation?
R: Yes, we do. We have booked a table for four.
S: May I have the name, please?
R: The name is Reynolds.
S: Yes, madam. One moment, please. I'm afraid there's no table reservation marked in that name, madam.
R: But I called myself only this afternoon and I was promised a window table.

S: I see. There must be some mistake, madam.
R: Then what's to be done?
S: Ah, we could give you a pleasant table in the Jingtai Room, though it is not a window table.
R: Well, I suppose we will have to manage with that, but I must tell you I'm disappointed with your service.
S: I'm sorry indeed that this should have happened. But I assure you we will make every effort to make your evening here a pleasant one.
R: We do wish to enjoy your good service.

Additional Exercises:

Divide the class into groups. Each group makes a situational dialogue using words or phrases for dealing with complaints You may refer to the working procedures or sentence patterns in Dialogue 1, Dialogue 2, Dialogue 3 and Dialogue 4.

Part Five   Consolidation
五、巩固练习

A A Survey about Customer Service

As a server in the hotel, one might be dealing with 10 or 100 customers a day. Whether the interaction between you and your customer is a positive or negative one largely depends on the way you react to their demand or complaint. Take this quiz to find out if you can offer good services to the customer in your hotel.

1) You should greet and say the name of the hotel when you answer the phone.
   ○ True   ○ False
2) Your clothes matter when dealing face to face with customers.
   ○ True   ○ False
3) You should tell the customer if he/she is at fault.
   ○ True   ○ False
4) Argue with the customer. Stand for your right.
   ○ True   ○ False
5) Apologize to the customer even if the fault was done by another staff.
   ○ True   ○ False
6) When shaking hands, your hand should go soft and let the other party squeeze it.
   ○ True   ○ False
7) Feedback by clients or customers is not important.
   ○ True   ○ False

8) We must put ourselves in the customers' shoes if they lodge a complaint.
   ○ True   ○ False
9) Repeat customer's complaint after they have said it to be sure.
   ○ True   ○ False
10) Give away name cards with only one hand.
    ○ True   ○ False

B Translation

i. Translate the following sentences into Chinese.
1. I'm terribly sorry for that. I can give you something else if you'd like. That will be on the house (免费赠送), of course.
2. We do apologize for the inconvenience. I'll have toilet items(浴室备品) sent to your room immediately.
3. I'm sorry to have caused you such inconvenience. I assure (保证)you such things won't happen again. Thank you for telling us.
4. Indeed, we regret very much for not being able to comply with (满足)your request.
5. I'm sorry. It's the policy of our hotel. I hope you will understand(理解).

ii. Translate the following sentences into English.
1. 我昨晚整夜没合眼(a wink of sleep)，蚊子骚扰(pester)了我一夜。
2. 对不起，牛排烧煳了。您是不是吃点别的什么，当然这是酒店的一点心意(compliments)。
3. 我受到一个男服务员无礼对待(badly treated)，他会毁了(ruin)你们酒店的名声。
4. 很抱歉听您这么说，请相信我们一定会调查(look into)此事，尽快给您回复。
5. 对不起，先生，劝您别这样做，这是违反我们规定的(against our regulations)。

C Writing

A Letter of Complaint 投诉信

Travel is a kind of special lifestyle consisting of accommodation, food and beverage, transportation, communication and so on. As soon as the guests check in, all the related departments of a hotel need to work together to supply them the proper goods and services. If guests are not content with the services offered by the hotel, they will certainly complain.

Generally, complaints can be expressed in two different ways, by telephone, or by letter. A complaint may be sent directly to the related departments or to the General Manager. After receiving the complaints, the hotel should look into the matter; then take appropriate measures to handle the complaints.

Suppose you are the General Manager of Crowne Plaza Hotel, write a reply to the letter of complaint forwarded by Jane Clinton who is disappointed to receive poor service during her stay with your hotel.

Outline:

1. Your apologies and sympathies
2. Measures you will take
3. Compensation you will make
4. Your wish to offer better service

Crowne Plaza Hotel
No. 17, 4th Block, 1st Ring Road,
Hangzhou, Zhejiang

Attn: Mr. Lin Yunzhi
Dear Mr. Lin,

    As one of your regular guests, I'm writing to complain about my stay with your hotel.

    To be frank, I am terribly disappointed at your service as well as your hotel facilities. Firstly, when I checked in your receptionists chatted aloud. I waited for almost twenty minutes before my luggage was sent up to my room. Moreover, the tap was out of order when I took a shower. Worst of all, the hotel failed to provide us with room service the next morning. I find it unacceptable that you sold us a room that was not similar to the description on your website, and therefore I claim a refund of RMB 800.

    I sincerely hope that you could look into this matter and the problems mentioned above can be solved at your earliest convenience.

Yours sincerely,
Jane Clinton

Appendices 附　录

Appendix 1

客房设施和日用品

towel 毛巾
bath towel 浴巾
face towel 小方巾
bath mat 地巾
shampoo 洗发水
conditioner 护发素
toothbrush 牙刷
toothpaste 牙膏

curtain 窗帘
clothes-hanger 衣架
pillow 枕头
pillow case 枕袋
throw pillow 抱枕
quilt 被子

coffee table 茶几
bed-head 床头
electric kettle 电热水壶
sewing kit 针线包
folder 文件夹
writing paper 信纸
envelope 信封
wardrobe 衣柜
drawer 抽屉
vanity/dressing table 梳妆台
breakfast card 早餐卡
ashtray 烟灰缸
shoes board 鞋拔子
shoe basket 鞋筐
iron 熨斗
ironing board 熨衣板
floor lamp 落地灯
table light 台灯

tissues 面巾纸
toilet paper 卫生纸
comb 梳子
bath tub 浴缸
toilet bowl 马桶
bath robe 浴袍
hairdryer 吹风机
cotton ball 棉球

blanket 毛毯
extra bed 加床
hard mattress 硬床垫
soft mattress 软床垫
bed cover 床罩
sheet 床单

adapter 插头
extension code 接线板
transformer 变压器
switch board 控制板
safe 保险箱
bedside table 床头柜
door bell 门铃
door handle 门把手
door knob 门把手
door stopper 门堵
king bed 双人床
TV remote control 电视遥控器
rubbish bin 垃圾桶
flash light 手电筒
key hole 取电器
wall lamp 壁灯
data line 数据线
peep hole 门镜猫眼

shower head 喷头
tap 水龙头
soap dish 皂碟
rubber mat 防滑垫
shower curtains 浴帘
wash basin 面盆
towel rail 毛巾架
slippers 拖鞋

quilt cover 被罩
bed skirting 床裙
laundry list 洗衣单
laundry bag 洗衣袋

lamp shade 灯罩
No Smoking Card 请勿吸烟卡
scissors 剪刀
alarm clock 闹钟
shoe shine mitt/paper 擦鞋布
candy bottle 糖果盅
safety chain 安全链
mini bar 小酒吧
tissue paper box 面巾纸盒
note pad 便签
sanitary bag 卫生袋
bed pad 床垫子
bed head board 床头板
shopping bag 购物袋
sheer curtain 纱帘
key insert 取电器

Appendix 2

中餐英文菜名

冷菜类 Cold Dishes

拌豆腐丝：Shredded Tofu with Sauce
白切鸡：Boiled Chicken with Sauce
拌双耳：Tossed Black and White Fungus
冰梅凉瓜：Bitter Melon in Plum Sauce
冰镇芥兰：Chinese Broccoli with Wasabi
朝鲜辣白菜：Korean Cabbage in Chili Sauce
朝鲜泡菜：Kimchi
川北凉粉：Clear Noodles in Chili Sauce
刺身凉瓜：Bitter Melon with Wasabi
豆豉多春鱼：Shisamo in Black Bean Sauce
夫妻肺片：Pork Lungs in Chili Sauce
干拌牛舌：Ox Tongue in Chili Sauce
干拌顺风：Pig Ear in Chili Sauce
老醋泡花生：Peanuts Pickled in Aged Vinegar
凉拌金针菇：Golden Mushrooms and Mixed Vegetables
凉拌西芹云耳：Celery with White Fungus
卤水大肠：Marinated Pork Intestines
卤水鸭肉：Marinated Duck Meat
萝卜干毛豆：Dried Radish with Green Soybean
麻辣肚丝：Shredded Pig Tripe in Chili Sauce
泡菜什锦：Assorted Pickles
泡椒凤爪：Chicken Feet with Pickled Peppers
珊瑚笋尖：Sweet and Sour Bamboo Shoots
爽口西芹：Crispy Celery
跳水木耳：Black Fungus with Pickled Capsicum
拌海螺：Whelks and Cucumber
五香牛肉：Spicy Roast Beef
五香熏干：Spicy Smoked Dried Tofu
五香熏鱼：Spicy Smoked Fish
腌三文鱼：Marinated Salmon
酸辣瓜条：Cucumber with Hot and Sour Sauce
拌茄泥：Mashed Eggplant with Garlic
糖蒜：Sweet Garlic
凉拌黄瓜：Cucumber in Sauce

热菜类 Hot Dishes
猪肉类 Pork

白菜豆腐焖酥肉：Braised Pork Cubes with Tofu and Chinese Cabbage
鲍鱼红烧肉：Braised Pork with Abalone
川味小炒：Shredded Pork with Vegetables, Sichuan Style
地瓜烧肉：Stewed Diced Pork and Sweet Potatoes
东坡方肉：Braised Dongpo Pork
冬菜扣肉：Braised Pork with Preserved Vegetables
方竹笋炖肉：Braised Pork with Bamboo Shoots
红烧狮子头：Stewed Pork Ball in Brown Sauce
脆皮乳猪：Crispy BBQ Suckling Pig
回锅肉片：Sautéed Sliced Pork with Pepper and Chili
木耳肉片：Sautéed Sliced Pork with Black Fungus
京酱肉丝：Sautéed Shredded Pork in Sweet Bean Sauce
什菌炒红烧肉：Sautéed Diced Pork with Assorted Mushrooms
孜然寸骨：Sautéed Spare Ribs with Cumin
火爆腰花：Sautéed Pig's Kidney
腊肉炒香芹：Sautéed Preserved Pork with Celery
咖喱肉：Curry Pork
罗汉肚：Pork Tripe Stuffed with Meat
清炸里脊：Deep-Fried Pork Filet
软炸里脊：Soft-Fried Pork Filet
尖椒里脊丝：Fried Shredded Pork Filet with Hot Pepper
滑溜里脊片：Quick-Fried Pork Filet Slices with Sauce
银芽肉丝：Sautéed Shredded Pork with Bean Sprouts
蒜香烩肥肠：Braised Pork Intestines with Mashed Garlic
芽菜回锅肉：Sautéed Sliced Pork with Scallion and Bean Sprouts
蚂蚁上树：Sautéed Vermicelli with Spicy Minced Pork
芹菜肉丝：Sautéed Shredded Pork with Celery
青椒肉丝：Sautéed Shredded Pork with Green Pepper
红烧蹄筋：Braised Pig Tendon in Brown Sauce
清蒸猪脑：Steamed Pig Brains
芋头蒸排骨：Steamed Spare Ribs with Taro
蝴蝶骨：Braised Spare Ribs
腊肉红菜苔：Sautéed Preserved Pork with Red Vegetables
竹筒腊肉：Steamed Preserved Pork in Bamboo Tube

盐煎肉：Fried Pork Slices with Salted Pepper

蛋黄狮子头：Stewed Meat Ball with Egg Yolk

牛肉类 Beef

爆炒牛肋骨：Sautéed Beef Ribs
彩椒牛柳：Sautéed Beef Filet with Bell Peppers
白灼肥牛：Scalded Beef
菜胆蚝油牛肉：Sautéed Sliced Beef and Vegetables in Oyster Sauce
菜心扒牛肉：Grilled Beef with Shanghai Greens
川北牛尾：Braised Oxtail in Chili Sauce, Sichuan Style
川汁牛柳：Sautéed Beef Filet in Chili Sauce, Sichuan Style
葱爆肥牛：Sautéed Beef with Scallion
黑椒牛柳：Sautéed Beef Filet with Black Pepper
黑椒牛柳粒：Sautéed Diced Beef Filet with Black Pepper
铁板串烧牛肉：Sizzling Beef Kebabs
铁板木瓜牛仔骨：Sizzling Calf Ribs with Papaya
中式牛柳：Beef Filet with Tomato Sauce, Chinese Style
中式牛排：Beef Steak with Tomato Sauce, Chinese Style
孜然烤牛肉：Grilled Beef with Cumin
孜然辣汁焖牛腩：Braised Beef Brisket with Cumin
家乡小炒肉：Sautéed Beef Filet, Country Style
青豆牛肉粒：Sautéed Diced Beef with Green Beans
豉油牛肉：Steamed Beef in Black Bean Sauce
什菜牛肉：Sautéed Beef with Mixed Vegetables
鱼香牛肉：Yu-Shiang Beef（Sautéed with Spicy Garlic Sauce）
芥兰牛肉：Sautéed Beef with Chinese Broccoli
雪豆牛肉：Sautéed Beef with Snow Peas
青椒牛肉：Sautéed Beef with Pepper and Onions
陈皮牛肉：Beef with Dried Orange Peel
干烧牛肉：Dry-Braised Shredded Beef, Sichuan Style
西兰花牛柳：Stir-Fried Beef Filet with Broccoli
铁锅牛柳：Braised Beef Filet in Iron Pot
干煸牛柳丝：Sautéed Shredded Beef
沾水牛肉：Boiled Beef
牛肉炖土豆：Braised Beef with Potatoes
清蛋牛肉：Fried Beef with Scrambled Eggs
米粉牛肉：Steamed Beef with Rice Flour
咖喱蒸牛肚：Steamed Ox Tripe with Curry

禽蛋类 Poultry and Eggs

巴蜀小炒鸡：Sautéed Chicken with Hot and Green Pepper
板栗焖仔鸡：Braised Chicken with Chestnuts
川味红汤鸡：Chicken in Hot Spicy Sauce, Sichuan Style
脆皮鸡：Crispy Chicken
大千鸡片：Sautéed Sliced Chicken
大煮干丝：Braised Shredded Chicken with Ham and Dried Tofu
当红炸子鸡：Deep-Fried Chicken
干锅鸡：Griddle Cooked Chicken with Pepper
干锅鸡胗：Griddle Cooked Chicken Gizzard
宫保鸡丁：Kung Pao Chicken
啤酒鸡：Stewed Chicken in Beer
飘香手撕鸡：Poached Sliced Chicken
四川辣子鸡：Sautéed Diced Chicken with Chili and Pepper, Sichuan Style
酥炸鸡胸：Deep-Fried Crispy Chicken Breast
铁板豆豉鸡：Sizzling Chicken in Black Bean Sauce
腰果鸡丁：Sautéed Diced Chicken and Cashew Nuts
一品蒜花鸡：Deep-Fried Chicken with Garlic
怪味鸡丝：Special Flavored Shredded Chicken
口水鸡：Steamed Chicken with Chili Sauce
清蒸童子鸡：Steamed Spring Chicken
贵妃鸡：Chicken Wings and Legs with Brown Sauce
江南百花鸡：Steamed Chicken Skin with Shrimp Paste
道口烧鸡：Red-Cooked Chicken, Daokou Style
金钱鸡：Grilled Ham and Chicken
芝麻鸡：Boiled Chicken with Sesame and Spicy Sauce
叫化鸡：Beggars Chicken（Baked Chicken）
一鸡三吃：A Chicken Prepared in Three Ways
青椒鸭肠：Stir-Fried Duck Intestines with Green Pepper
糟溜鸭三白：Stewed and Seasoned Duck Slices, Duck Feet and Duck Liver
四川樟茶鸭（配荷叶饼）：Smoked Duck, Sichuan Style（with Lotus-Leaf-Like Pancake）
虫草炖老鸭：Stewed Duck with Aweto
罗汉扒大鸭：Braised Duck with Mixed Vegetables
川式煎鹅肝：Fried Goose Liver, Sichuan Style
冬草花炖鹧鸪：Stewed Quail with Aweto
脆皮乳鸽：Crispy Pigeon
吊烧乳鸽王：Roast Pigeon

天麻炖乳鸽: Stewed Pigeon with Gastrodia Tuber
荷包蛋: Poached Egg

韭菜炒鸡蛋: Scrambled Egg with Leek
葱花炒鸡蛋: Scrambled Egg with Scallion

海鲜类 Seafood

鲍鱼烧牛头: Braised Abalone with Ox Head
红烧鲍翅燕: Braised Abalone, Shark's Fin and Bird's Nest
红烧鲍鱼: Braised Abalone
鲍汁葱烧辽参: Braised Sea Cucumber in Abalone Sauce
北极贝刺身: Scallops Sashimi
碧绿鲜带子: Braised Scallops with Vegetables
宫保鲜带子: Kung Pao Scallops
鸽蛋烧裙边: Braised Turtle Rim with Pigeon Egg
姜葱酥炸生蚝: Deep-Fried Oyster with Ginger and Scallion
干煎带鱼: Deep-Fried Ribbonfish
清蒸桂鱼: Steamed Mandarin Fish
松鼠桂鱼: Sweet and Sour Mandarin Fish
木瓜腰豆煮海参: Braised Sea Cucumber with Kidney Beans and Papaya
红烧小黄鱼豆腐: Braised Small Yellow Croakers and Tofu
锅仔雪菜鲈鱼: Stewed Perch with Potherb Mustard
红烧甲鱼: Braised Turtle in Brown Sauce
香辣蟹: Sautéed Crab in Hot Spicy Sauce
家乡鳝鱼: Sautéed Eel with Hot and Green Pepper
干烧大虾: Dry-Braised Prawn with Ham and Asparagus
麻婆龙虾仔: Mapo Baby Lobster（Braised in Chili Sauce）
清炒水晶河虾仁: Sautéed Shelled River Shrimps
水晶虾仁: Sautéed Shelled Shrimps
蒜茸蒸大虾: Steamed Prawns with Garlic
泰式辣椒炒虾仁: Sautéed Shrimps with Chili, Thai Style
鲜果沙律虾: Prawn Salad with Fresh Fruits
鲜豌豆炒河虾仁: Sautéed Shrimps with Fresh Beans
香葱白果虾: Sautéed Shrimps with Gingko and Scallion
滋补砂锅大虾: Boiled King Prawns en Casserole

Appendix 3

西餐英文菜名

头盘及沙拉类

Smoked Salmon 腌熏三文鱼
Marinated Salmon with Lemon and Capers 腌三文鱼
Caesar Salad 凯撒沙拉
Chicken Liver Terrine with Morels 鲜蘑鸡肝批
Baked Stuffed Crab Shell 奶酪瓤蟹盖
Seafood Salad with Fresh Fruit 鲜果海鲜沙拉
Chef's Salad 厨师沙拉
Tuna Fish Salad 金枪鱼沙拉
Salad Nicoise 尼斯沙拉

汤类

Cream of Mushroom Soup 奶油蘑菇汤
Cream of Carrot Soup 奶油胡萝卜汤
Cream of Asparagus Soup 奶油芦笋汤
Traditional Tomato Soup 番茄浓汤
Seafood Chowder 海鲜周打汤
French Onion Soup 法式洋葱汤
Beef Consomme 牛肉清汤
Hungarian Beef Goulash 匈牙利浓汤
Oxtail Soup 香浓牛尾汤
Minestrone Soup 意大利蔬菜汤
Hearty Lentil Soup 蔬菜干豆汤
Chilled Avocado Soup 牛油梨冻汤
Gazpacho 西班牙番茄冻汤

禽类

Braised Goose Liver in Red Wine 红酒鹅肝
Chicken Cordon Bleu 奶酪火腿鸡排
Grilled Stuffed Chicken Rolls 烧瓤春鸡卷
Braised Chicken with Red Wine 红酒烩鸡
Baked Chicken Breast Stuffed with Mushrooms and Cheese 烤鸡胸酿奶酪蘑菇馅
Deep-Fried Chicken and Bacon Rolls 炸培根鸡肉卷
Poached Chicken Breast with Balsamico Sauce 水波鸡胸配意式香醋汁
Roast Turkey with Cranberry Sauce 烤火鸡配红浆果少司
Roast Stuffed Turkey 烤瓤火鸡
Barbecued Chicken Leg 烧烤鸡腿
Roasted Lemon Marinade Chicken Leg with French Fries 烤柠檬鸡腿配炸薯条
Char-Grilled Chicken Breast 扒鸡胸
Chicken Curry 咖喱鸡
Pan-fried Duck Breast with Sautéed Potatoes and Truffles 秘制鸭胸配黑菌炒土豆

牛肉类

Stewed Beef 红烩牛肉
Fricasseed Veal 白烩小牛肉
Grilled Beef Tenderloin with Black Pepper Sauce 牛里脊扒配黑椒少司
Grilled Beef Rib-Eye Steak 扒肉眼牛排
Roast Beef Sirloin Steak with Red Wine Sauce 西冷牛排配红酒少司
T-Bone Steak T骨牛扒
Roast Beef 烤牛肉
Beef Tenderloin and Goose Liver with Truffle and Port Wine Sauce 罗西尼牛柳配苯酒汁
Beef Tenderloin Steak with Green Peppercorn Sauce 青椒汁牛柳
Sizzling Sirloin Steak 铁板西冷牛扒
Pan-fried Veal Steak Oscar with Hollandaise Sauce 香煎奥斯卡仔排
Beef Curry 咖喱牛肉
Fillet Steak Wellington 威灵顿牛柳
Beef Stroganoff 俄式牛柳丝
Braised Ox-Tongue 烩牛舌
Osso Bucco 红烩牛膝
Venison Fillet Black Pepper Coat with Wild Mushroom and Celery Brick 黑胡椒鹿柳配野蘑菇和芹菜烤面皮

猪肉类

Barbecued Spare Ribs 烧烤排骨
Smoked Spare Ribs with Honey 烟熏蜜汁肋排
Pork Piccatta 意大利米兰猪排
Stuffed Pork Roulade with Yellow Peach Sauce 瓤馅猪肉卷配黄桃汁
Pan-fried Swiss Meat Loaf with Pesto Sauce 煎面包肠香草汁
Deep-Fried Pork Chop 炸猪排

羊肉类

Grilled Lamb Chop 扒羊排
Grilled New Zealand Lamb Chop 扒新西兰羊排
Roast Lamb Chop with Cheese and Red Wine Sauce 烤羊排配奶酪和红酒汁
Lamb Kebabs 羊肉串
Roasted Mutton Leg 烤羊腿

鱼和海鲜类

Seafood Kebabs 海鲜串
Grilled Tuna Steak 扒金枪鱼
Grilled Norwegian Salmon Fillet 扒挪威三文鱼排
Grilled Salmon with Lime Butter 三文鱼扒配青柠黄油
Braised Sole Fillet & Sea Scallops with Red Wine and Walnuts 比目鱼柳和扇贝配红酒核桃汁
Pan-fried Whole Sole 煎比目鱼
Roasted Salmon Fillet with Pesto Black Olive Purée 烤三文鱼柳配香草汁和黑橄榄酱
Roasted Salmon Steak with Tagliatelle & Saffron Sauce 烤三文鱼排意大利宽面和藏红花汁
Grilled Red Snapper Fillet 红加吉鱼排
Grilled Fish Fillet in Lemon Butter Sauce 黄油柠檬汁扒鱼柳
Grille King Prawns 扒大虾
Grilled King Prawns with Garlic Herb Butter 蒜茸大虾
Baked Lobster with Garlic Butter 巴黎黄油烤龙虾
Gratinated Lobster in Mornay Sauce 奶酪汁龙虾
Deep-Fried Squid Rings 香炸西班牙鱿鱼圈
Gratinated Mussels Hollandaise Sauce 荷兰汁青口贝

蛋类

Fried Eggs with Ham 火腿煎蛋
Quiche Lorraine 洛林乳蛋饼
Scrambled Eggs 熘糊蛋

面、粉及配菜类

Macaroni with Seafood 海鲜通心粉
Spaghetti with Seafood 海鲜意粉
Cheese Lasagna 意大利奶酪千层饼
Pizza Vegetarian 什莱奶酪比萨饼
Seafood Pizza 海鲜比萨
Roast Beef and Mushroom Pizza 烤牛肉蘑菇比萨
Spaghetti Bolognaise 肉酱意大利粉
Cheese Ravioli in Herbed Cream Sauce 意大利奶酪馄饨
Stir-Fried Seafood Rice with Curry 咖喱海鲜炒饭
Saffron Rice 红花饭
Paella 西班牙海鲜饭
Beef Burger 牛肉汉堡包
Chicken Burger 鸡肉汉堡包
American Hot Dog 美式热狗
Club Sandwich 俱乐部三文治
Tuna Fish Sandwich 金枪鱼三文治
Roasted Beef Sandwich 烤牛肉三文治
Healthy Sandwich 健康三文治
Smoked Salmon 烟熏三文鱼
Mashed Potatoes 土豆泥
Lyonnaise Potatoes 里昂那土豆
Duchesse Potatoes 公爵夫人土豆
Braised Red Cabbage with Apple 烩红椰菜

甜品

Black Forest Cake 黑森林蛋糕
English Fruit Cake 英式水果蛋糕
Strawberry Cheese Cake 草莓奶酪蛋糕
Strawberry Cake 草莓蛋糕
Blueberry Cheese Cake 蓝莓奶酪蛋糕
American Cheese Cake 美式奶酪蛋糕
Green Tea Cheese Cake 绿茶奶酪蛋糕
Italian Tiramisu 意大利提拉米苏
Marble Cheese Cake 大理石奶酪蛋糕
Coffee Cheese Cake 咖啡奶酪蛋糕
Cranberry Muffin 红莓松糕
Mixed Nuts Pie 干果派
Blueberry Muffin 蓝莓松糕
Linzer Cake 琳泽蛋糕
Mango Mousse Cake 芒果木司蛋糕
Apple Pie 苹果派
Strawberry Napoleon Sliced 草莓酥条
Chocolate Hazelnut Cake 巧克力榛子蛋糕
Chocolate Mousse 巧克力木司
Puff Pastry with Fruits 水果脆皮酥盒
Sacher Cake 维也纳巧克力蛋糕
Passion Mousse 热情果木司
Almond Donuts 杏仁多纳圈
Milk Chocolate Donuts 牛奶巧克力多纳圈
Fruit with Sabayon 鲜水果配沙巴洋
Fresh Fruit Tart 水果蛋挞
White Chocolate Brulee 白巧克力奶油布丁
Green Tea Pudding 绿茶布丁
Mango Pudding 芒果布丁
Warm Sticky Date Pudding 热枣布丁
Vanilla Pudding 香草布丁
Cream Caramel / Caramel Custard 焦糖布丁
Walnut Brownies 果仁布朗尼
Coffee Opera Slice 咖啡剧本蛋糕

饼干及其他

Lady Finger 手指饼
Butterfly Cracker 蝴蝶酥
Chocolate Cookies 巧克力曲奇
Popcorn(Sweet/Salt) 爆米花(甜/咸)
Vanilla Ice Cream 香草冰淇淋
Chocolate Ice Cream 巧克力冰淇淋
Strawberry Ice Cream 草莓冰淇淋
Green Tea Ice Cream 绿茶冰淇淋
Sherbets 冰霜
Strawberry Milk Shake 草莓奶昔
Chocolate Milk Shake 巧克力奶昔
Coffee Milk Shake 咖啡奶昔

面包类

Fruit Danish 水果丹麦
Croissant 牛角包
Pita Bread Plain 袋子包
Farmer Bread 农夫包
Onion Loaf 洋葱包
Whole Wheat Bread 全麦包
Soft Roll 软包
Hard Roll 硬包
French Baguette 长法棍
Toast 吐司面包

Appendix 4

外国酒名

Wine 葡萄酒

Chardonnay 霞多丽	Sauvignon Blanc 长相思	Syrah 西拉
Cabernet 赤霞珠	Riesling 雷司令	Silvaner 西万尼
Merlot 梅洛	Carignan 佳丽酿	Bordeaux 波尔多
Pinot Noir 黑皮诺	Ruby Cabernet 宝石解百纳	Traminer 琼瑶浆
Lafite 拉菲	Sangiovese 桑娇维赛	

Cocktails 鸡尾酒

Long Island Iced Tea 长岛冰茶	Sex on the Beach 激情海岸	Blue Hawaiian 蓝色夏威夷
Margherita 玛格丽特	Mojito 莫吉托	Singapore Sling 新加坡司令
Cosmopolitan 大都会	Bloody Mary 血腥玛丽	Manhattan 曼哈顿
Tequila Sunrise 龙舌兰日出	White Russian 白俄罗斯	Summer Punch 夏日宾治
Mai Tai 美态	Gin and Tonic 金汤力	Pink Lady 红粉佳人
Strawberry Daiquiri 草莓戴吉利酒	Gin Fizz 金菲士	Angel's Kiss 天使之吻
Pina Colada 椰林飘香	Mimosa 含羞草	

Beer 啤酒

Heineken 喜力	Grolsch 高仕	Suntory 三得利
Corona 科罗娜	Asahi 朝日	Budlight 百威淡啤
Budweiser 百威	Tiger 虎牌	
Carlsberg 嘉士伯	Blue Ribbon 蓝带	

Liquor 烈性酒

Belvedere 雪树	Captain Morgan 摩根船长	Martell 马爹利
Grey Goose 灰鹅	Don Quixote 堂吉诃德	Remy Martin 人头马
Stoli 苏联红	Jose Cuervo Gold 豪帅金快活	Mezcal 梅兹卡尔
Ketel One 坎特一号	Patron 培恩	Smirnoff 斯米尔诺夫/皇冠
Absolut 绝对	Hennessy 轩尼诗	Jack Daniel's 杰克丹尼
Bombay Sapphire 孟买蓝宝石	Johnnie Walker 尊尼获加	Bacardi 百加得
Malibu 马利宝	Chivas 芝华士	

Shots 短饮

Jaeger Bomb 雅格炸弹	Kamikaze 神风	Lemon Drop 柠檬糖果

Appendix 5

中国酒名

黄酒类 Yellow Wine

1. 8年香雕绍兴酒 Xiangdiao Shaoxing Medium Sweet (8 Years)
2. 陈年彩坛花雕 Caitan Huadiao Medium Sweet
3. 5年香雕绍兴酒 Xiangdiao Shaoxing(5 Years) Medium Sweet
4. 绍兴花雕10年 Shaoxing Huadiao(10 Years) Medium Sweet
5. 绍兴花雕20年 Shaoxing Huadiao (20 Years) Medium Sweet
6. 绍兴花雕及清酒 Shaoxing Huadiao and Sake Medium Sweet
7. 三十年花雕 Huadiao Shaoxing (30 Years) Medium Sweet
8. 绍兴加饭 Shaoxing Jiafan Medium Dry
9. 女儿红12年 Nu'er Hong (12 Years)
10. 女儿红18年 Nu'er Hong (18 Years)
11. 古越龙山 Guyue Longshan
12. 青瓷五年 Qingci Huadiao(5 Years) Medium Sweet

白酒类 Liquor

13. 北京醇 Beijing Chun
14. 二锅头 Erguotou(500ml 56°)
15. 红星二锅头52度 Red Star Erguotou (500ml 52°)
16. 古钟二锅头 Guzhong Erguotou(500ml 46°)
17. 蓝花珍品二锅头 Lanhua Zhenpin Erguotou
18. 红星珍品二锅头(500毫升52度) Red Star Zhenpin Erguotou (500ml 52°)
19. 牛栏山经典二锅头(500毫升52度) Niulanshan Jingdian Erguotou (500ml 52°)
20. 青瓷珍品二锅头 Qingci Zhenpin Erguotou(500ml 46°)
21. 京酒38度 Jing Jiu(500ml 38°)
22. 三品京酒(500毫升38度) Sanpin Jing Jiu (500ml 38°)
23. 三品京酒(500毫升52度) Sanpin Jing Jiu (500ml 52°)
24. 酒鬼38度 Jiu Gui(500ml 38°)
25. 酒鬼52度 Jiu Gui (500ml 52°)
26. 小酒鬼(250ml) Xiao Jiu Gui(250ml 38°)
27. 国酿(贵州茅台系列) Guo Niang (Moutai Liquor Series)
28. 茅台38度 Moutai (500ml 38°)
29. 茅台53度 Moutai (500ml 53°)
30. 茅台(三十年) Moutai (30 years)
31. 茅台(十五年) Moutai (15 years)
32. 贵州醇 Guizhou Chun
33. 国窖38度 Guo Jiao (500ml 38°)
34. 国窖52度 Guo Jiao (500ml 52°)
35. 国窖1573 Guo Jiao 1573 (The First Cellar in China)
36. 泸州老窖38度 Luzhou Lao Jiao(38°)
37. 泸州老窖52度 Luzhou Lao Jiao(52°)
38. 康雍乾御冠酒(400毫升50度) Kang Yong Qian Imperial Crown (400ml 50°)
39. 康雍乾御酒(450毫升50度) Kang Yong Qian (450ml 50°)

40. 剑南春 38 度 Jiannanchun（38°）
41. 剑南春 52 度 Jiannanchun（52°）
42. 蒙古王 44 度 Mongolian King（44°）
43. 三星金六福（高．低）Jinliufu Three-Star (High/Low)
44. 三星金六福（三两）Jinliufu (150ml)
45. 五星金六福（高．低）Jinliufu Five-Star (High, Low)
46. 金六福（五星）52 度 Jinliufu (Five-Star) (52°)
47. 水井坊 39 度 Shuijingfang (39°)
48. 水井坊 52 度 Shuijingfang (52°)
49. 水井坊 53 度 Shuijingfang (53°)
50. 五粮液 39 度 Wuliangye (39°)
51. 五粮液 52 度 Wuliangye (52°)
52. 五粮液一帆风顺 52 度 Wuliangye Liquor Yi Fan Feng Shun (52°)—Symbolizing Plain Sailing
53. 小糊涂仙 52 度 Xiaohutuxian (52°)
54. 小角楼 Xiaojiaolou

啤酒 Beer
55. 青岛啤酒 Tsing Tao Beer
56. 青岛扎啤/青岛生啤 Tsing Tao Draught
57. 燕京啤酒 Yanjing Beer
58. 燕京生啤 0.3 升 Yanjing Draught (0.3L)
59. 燕京无醇啤酒 Yanjing Alcohol-Free
60. 燕京扎啤 Yanjing Draught
61. 雪花啤酒 Snow Beer
62. 北京生啤 Beijing Draught Beer
63. 哈尔滨啤酒 Harbin Beer
64. 百威啤酒 Budweiser
65. 嘉士伯啤酒 Carlsberg
66. 喜力 Heineken
67. 朝日啤酒 Asahi Beer
68. 老虎啤酒 Tiger
69. 蓝带啤酒 Blue Ribbon

葡萄酒 Wine
70. 92 年长城干红葡萄酒 Great Wall Red Wine (Year 1992)
71. 92 年张裕卡斯特干红 Changyu Castel (Year 1992)
72. 95 年张裕卡斯特干红 Changyu Castel (Year 1995)
73. 张裕解百纳干红葡萄酒 Changyu Cavernet
74. 张裕香槟 Changyu Sparkling Cider
75. 长城 1995（长城红葡萄酒，中国）Great Wall Cabernet Sauvignon (Year 1995)
76. 长城 2002（长城红葡萄酒，中国）Great Wall Cabernet Sauvignon (Year 2002)
77. 长城 A 区（长城红葡萄酒，中国）Great Wall Cabernet Sauvignon
78. 华夏 95 年长城 Great Wall Vintage Red Wine (Year 1995)
79. 华夏长城赤霞珠 Great Wall Cabernet Sauvignon Red Wine

80. 华夏长城葡萄园A区 Great Wall Region A Red Wine
81. 华夏长城莎当妮 Great Wall Chardonnay White Wine
82. 华夏长城特选 Great Wall Selection Red Wine
83. 沙城长城干红三星 Great Wall Dry Red (Three-Star)
84. 沙城长城干红四星 Great Wall Dry Red (Four-Star)
85. 沙城长城干红五星 Great Wall Dry Red (Five-Star)
86. 沙城长城干红一星 Great Wall Dry Red (One-Star)
87. 雷司令（龙徽，中国）Dragon Seal Riesling
88. 龙徽赤霞珠 Dragon Seal Cabernet Sauvignon Red Wine
89. 龙徽干白 Dragon Seal Dry White
90. 龙徽干白葡萄酒 Dragon Seal Dry White
91. 龙徽干红葡萄酒 Dragon Seal Dry Red
92. 龙徽怀来珍藏 Dragon Seal Huailai Reserve
93. 龙徽怀来珍藏干红葡萄酒 Dragon Seal Huailai Dry Red Reserve
94. 龙徽汽酒 Dragon Seal Sparkling Wine
95. 龙徽莎当妮 Dragon Seal Chardonnay White Wine
96. 龙徽庄园 Dragon Seal Cru de Red Wine
97. 龙徽庄园干红葡萄酒 Dragon Seal Cru de Dry Red
98. 西夏王冰白 Xixia King Ice Wine
99. 西夏王干红 Xixia King Dry Red
100. 西夏王世纪 Xixia King Red Wine
101. 总统特选南澳设拉子干红 President's Selection Shiraz Dry Red
102. 总统特选南澳莎当妮干白 President's Selection Chardonnay Dry White
103. 王朝干红 Dynasty Dry Red
104. 王朝干白 Dynasty Dry White

Appendix 6

中国茶和茶具

一、中国茶名

1. 绿茶：Green Tea

Lvmaofeng Tea 绿毛峰
Xihu Longjing Tea (Green Tea) 西湖龙井
Maojian Tea (Green Tea) 毛尖茶
Biluochun Tea (Green Tea) 碧螺春
Taiping Houkui Tea (Green Tea) 太平猴魁

Xinyang Maojian Tea (Green Tea) 信阳毛尖
Junshan Silver Needle Tea 君山银针
White Milli-Silver Needle Tea 大白毫
Yellow Mountain Fuzz Tip 黄山毛峰

2. 红茶：Black Tea

Keemun Black Tea 祁门红茶
Darjeeling Tea 大吉岭茶
Earl Grey Tea 伯爵茶
Mint Tea 薄荷锡兰茶
Assorted Chinese Herbal Tea 八宝茶

Lavender Tea 薰衣草茶
Greengage Black Tea 梅子红茶
Pu'er Tea 普洱
Aged Pu'er Tea 陈年普洱
31-Year Pu'er Tea 陈年普洱(31年)

3. 乌龙茶：Oolong Tea

Dahongpao Tea(Wuyi Mountain Rock Tea) 大红袍
Dongding Oolong Tea 冻顶乌龙
White Tipped Oolong 白毫乌龙

Taiwan Alishan Oolong Tea 台湾阿里山乌龙
Taiwan Ginsen Oolong Tea 台湾人参乌龙
Taiwan Cassia Oolong Tea 台湾桂花乌龙

4. 花茶：Scented Tea

Jasmine Tea 茉莉花茶
Chrysanthemum Tea 菊花茶

Jasmine Silver Needle Tea 茉莉大白毫
Peony Jasmine Tea 牡丹绣球

5. 茶饮料：Tea Drinks

Iced Black Tea / Iced Green Tea 冰红(绿)茶
Iced Milk Tea 冰奶茶
Hot Tea, HK Style 港式奶茶
Chocolate Milk Tea 巧克力奶茶
Iced Chocolate Milk Tea 冰巧克力奶茶
Strawberry Milk Tea 草莓奶茶
Peanut Milk Tea 花生奶茶
Hami Melon Milk Tea 哈密瓜奶茶
Coconut Milk Tea 椰香奶茶
Taro Milk Tea 芋香奶茶
Hot Lemon Tea 热柠檬茶

Iced Lemon Tea 冰柠檬茶
Pineapple Tea 菠萝果茶
Iced Pineapple Tea 菠萝冰茶
Iced Blackberry Tea 黑莓冰茶
Iced Strawberry Tea 草莓冰茶
Iced Blueberry Tea 蓝莓冰茶
Iced Mango Tea 芒果冰茶
Iced Peach Tea 蜜桃冰茶
Iced Kiwi Tea 奇异果冰茶
Pawpaw Milk Tea 木瓜奶茶

二、茶具名称

tea pot 茶壶
tea pad 壶垫
tea plate 茶船

tea pitcher 茶盅
lid saucer 盖置
tea serving tray 奉茶盘

tea cup 茶杯
cup saucer 杯托
tea towel tray 茶巾盘

tea holder 茶荷
tea towel 茶巾
tea brush 茶拂
timer 定时器
water heater 煮水器
water kettle 水壶
heating base 煮水器底座
tea cart 茶车
seat cushion 坐垫

cup cover 杯套
packing wrap 包壶巾
tea ware bag 茶具袋
ground pad 地衣
tea ware tray 茶托
strainer cup 同心杯
tea basin 水盂
brewing vessel 冲泡盅
covered bowl 盖碗

tea spoon 茶匙
tea ware 茶器
tea canister 茶罐
tea urn 茶瓮
tea table 茶桌
tea bowl 茶碗
spout bowl 有流茶碗

Appendix 7

中餐餐具

tea set 茶具
plate 盘子
dish 碟子
saucer 茶碟
bowl 碗
soup bowl 汤碗
soup plate 汤盘
soup cup 汤杯
dessert plate 点心盘
finger bowl 洗手盅
tray 托盘
table knife 餐刀

bread basket 面包蓝
sugar basin 糖罐
sugar tongs 方糖夹
milk jug 奶罐
table cloth/table linen 台布
napkin 餐巾
napkin ring 餐巾环
ice pot 水果冰淇淋杯
wine basket 酒蓝
chafing dish 酒精炉
rice bowl 饭碗
chopsticks 筷子

toothpick 牙签
cruet stand 调味品架
cruet 酱油醋瓶
black pepper ground 黑胡椒磨
mustard pot 芥末罐
tea spoon 茶勺
fruit knife 水果刀
fish knife 鱼刀
salt cellar, salt shaker 盐瓶
pepper bottle 胡椒面盆
ash-tray 烟缸
menu-holder 菜单架

Appendix 8

西餐餐具

dinner knife 主菜刀
dinner fork 主菜叉
soup spoon 汤勺
starter knife 头盆刀
starter fork 头盆叉
dessert fork 甜品叉
dessert spoon 甜品勺
butter knife 黄油刀

main course plate 主菜盆
soup plate 汤盆
tureen 汤盅
soup cup 汤杯
tray 托盘
service plate 装饰盘
starter plate 开胃品盘

table cloth mat 垫布
top cloth 装饰台布
apron 围嘴
table skirt 桌裙
service mat 托盘垫巾
pepper shaker 胡椒罐
waiter cleaning cloth 服务布巾

snail tongs 蜗牛夹
snail fork 蜗牛叉
cocktail fork 海鲜叉
lobster stick 龙虾签
lobster tong 龙虾钳
fish knife 鱼刀
fish fork 鱼叉
service fork 服务叉

dessert plate 甜点盘
bread plate 面包盘
butter dish 黄油碟
coffee set 咖啡具
coffee cup 咖啡杯
coffee spoon 咖啡勺
silver ware 银餐具

pantry cloth 抹布
chair cover 椅套
salt shaker 盐罐
candle stick 烛台
place card 席次卡
buffet warmer 自助餐保温锅
boiled stander 早餐蛋盅

corkscrew 开塞器
service spoon 服务勺
cake fork 蛋糕叉
steak knife 牛排刀
carving knife 切肉刀
sugar tong 糖夹
ice tong 冰夹
bottle opener 开瓶器

pitcher 冰水壶
wine basket 葡萄酒篮
ice water glass 冰水杯
white wine glass 白葡萄酒杯
red wine glass 红葡萄酒杯
champagne glass 香槟杯

service trolley 服务手推车
transfer trolley 送餐车
oven trolley 燃焰车
dessert trolley 甜品车
liqueur trolley 餐后酒车

Bibliography
参考文献

[1] Andrews, Sudhir. Hotel Front Office: A Training Manual (2nd ed) [M]. Tata McGraw-Hill, 2009.

[2] Baker, S. Principles of Hotel Front Office Operations (2nd ed) [M]. Cengage Learning EMEA, 2001.

[3] Bardi, J. James. Hotel Front Office Management (4th ed) [M]. John Wiley & Sons, Inc. 2007.

[4] Deveau, Linsley T., Patricia M. Deveau, Nestor de J. Portocarrero, and Marcel Escoffier. Front Office Management and Operations[M]. Prentice-Hall, Inc, 1996.

[5] Kappa, Margaret M., Aleta Nischke, and Patricia B. Schappert. Housekeeping Management. [M]. Educational Institute of the American Hotel & Lodging Association, 1997.

[6] Ismail, A. Front Office Operations and Management[M]. Thomson Delmar, 2002

[7] Bilbow, G. T. 朗文现代酒店业英语[M]. 北京：外语教学与研究出版社. 2005.

[8] 北京市人民政府外事办公室, 北京市民讲外语活动组委会办公室编著. 美食译苑：中文菜单英文译法[M]. 北京：世界知识出版社，2011.

[9] 郭兆康等. 宾馆英语[M]. 北京：高等教育出版社. 2003.

[10] 郭兆康等. 宾馆英语学习指导[M]. 北京：高等教育出版社，2004.

[11] 胡小平，郝海媛. 饭店管理专业英语[M]. 北京：对外经济贸易大学出版社，2006.

[12] 浩瀚. 酒店英语脱口秀[M]. 北京：北京师范大学出版社，2010.

[13] 李雪，李铁红，范宏博. 餐饮业职员英语口语大全[M]. 北京：机械工业出版社，2012.

[14] 刘海霞，张峥. 饭店英语360句[M]. 北京：旅游教育出版社，2008.

[15] 刘伟. 前厅与客房管理（第二版）[M]. 北京：高等教育出版社.2007 .

[16] 罗克特. 饭店英语情景口语100主题[M]. 北京：外文出版社，2009.

[17] 罗克特. 餐厅英语情景口语50主题[M]. 北京：外文出版社，2009.

[18] 柳玲，林晓珊等. 酒店服务行业实用英语对话及词汇手册[M]. 北京：中国水利水电出版社，2010.

[19] 韦斯利（Wesley, M.）著. 酒店英语[M]. 西安：世界图书出版公司，2009.

[20]《实用英语口语》教材编写组. 实用英语口语·旅游饭店篇[M]. 北京：北京理工大学出版社，2011.

[21] 邢怡. 餐饮英语[M]. 北京：高等教育出版社，2003.

[22] 袁露，阮蓓，李飞主编. 酒店英语[M]. 天津：天津大学出版社，2010.

[23] 朱华. 旅游英语视听说（第二版）[M]. 北京：北京大学出版社，2020.